INDIE GIRL

From Starting a Band to Launching a Fashion Company,
Nine Ways to Turn Your Creative Talent Into Reality

Arne Johnson & Karen Macklin

Illustrations by Michael Wertz

Foreword
Arne Johnson

Tired of waiting for someone to design the perfect skirt? Don't want to spend one more penny on an insulting spring break movie? Bored by the garbage that adults think makes great teen literature? Good—then you're on the right track. The next step is to take matters into your own hands.

It's easy to complain about all the junk out there posing as a genuine film or true art, but it's better to do something about it. Take me, for instance. I used to be a movie critic, and it was actually my job to complain about the latest wretched slasher about a bunch of teens getting killed while wandering around a campsite. Then one day I realized: If I want movies to be better, why not make one myself? Several years later, with no prior moviemaking experience, my best friend Shane and I filmed a documentary that's since been shown in theaters all around the country.

It wasn't difficult for us to get inspired after seeing our subjects. Our movie, Girls Rock!, is about a girls rock camp in Portland where seven-year-olds (yes, seven-year-olds!) form bands, write songs, learn to play instruments, and perform at a rock club for 700 screaming fans ... all in one week. If little Amelia could get her message out to the world, so could we—and so can you.

Thanks to modern technology, you can do most of the things that "world famous" artists do and probably do them better. This book will show you just how easy it is to make a TV show that puts Laguna Beach to shame, or how to make music that sounds better than all of those emo clones you hear on the modern rock station. Whether with sewing needle, hammer, or electric guitar, it's up to you to tell the world who you are—before it tells you who to be.

Karen Macklin

We hear about "girl power" all the time. It sounds great in theory. After all, when we are little girls, we know we rock. We know we're great writers, amazing story-tellers, and crafty designers. We have loads of ideas about who we want to be in the world and how to make it happen.

But then we get stuck along the way.

Someone tells us we can't do something, and we believe them. We start to hear about all of the things that men are supposedly better at—driving, building, fixing things, managing projects—and we believe that, too. Then, before you know it, we start confining ourselves to our mall excursions, our gossip sessions, and our tabloid magazines about dumb, rich celebrities. Ugh.

We can't accomplish our dreams by spending all of our free time getting our hair done, obsessing over our silhouettes, or crying over guys. And we certainly can't get anywhere by competing with each other. Real girl power (and that's for girls of ALL ages) is about coming together to make stuff happen. Period.

There is something magical about women working together to make music, put on a play, or invent a new style of fashion that's for girls who actually eat. I have worked for years as a writer, editor, and theater artist, and I have never felt more empowered than when I am working on a creative project with a group of cool girls. Any thoughts of insecurity, competition, jealousy, and doubt vanish because we are focused only on the art.

When we join forces, there is literally nothing we can't do. Use a power tool? Yup. Jam on a guitar? Definitely. Erect stage scenery? Choreograph a dance? Write, edit, and illustrate an entire magazine? Yes, yes, and yes.

This book is here to get you and your girl crew (and perhaps your guy friends, too!) started on all kinds of ambitious artistic endeavors. Because once you know the ropes, all you have to do is climb.

1 start a BAND · · · · · · · · · · · · · · · · 8

2 publish a ZINE · · · · · · · · · · · · 22

3 put on a PLAY · · · · · · · · · · · · · 36

4 film a TV SHOW · · · · · · · · · · · · 54

5 create an ART EXHIBIT · · · · 70

6 form a DANCE TROUPE ····· 84

launch a FASHION
COMPANY ···················· 96

8 hold a POETRY SLAM ····· 110

9 make a PARADE ·········· 124

1 start a BAND

"In our history, as an all-female band, we have faced some discrimination in the music business. Before we would play shows people would ask us if we were the girlfriends of the band playing, or if we actually played our instruments. Sometimes the assumption is made that other people write our music or that we don't have a hand in the business side of things. By self-managing, booking our tours, and writing our own music we hope to dispel some stereotypes in regard to women in music."

—**Mona Tavakoli**, drummer for Raining Jane

¡Rock!

It's hard to imagine a life without music. Music defines everything in our lives, from the clothes we wear to the posters tacked on our walls to the people we hang out with. And iPods, iTunes and iMboredWithRadio make surrounding ourselves in *someone else's* music really easy. But have you ever considered making your own?

A lot of people think music is something magical that only someone famous can make—that "normal" people don't have the skills to create melodies and rhythms on their own. **But the reality is that you don't need prodigal talent or a father named John Lennon to make great music. You just need soul—and a little motivation.**

The Beatles are a perfect example. This historically famous foursome, which most rock critics consider the greatest musical geniuses of all time, couldn't read a lick of music when they started out. They picked up chords by watching other bands and friends play. In fact, their arrangements are so simple that, if you have a basic knowledge of chords, you can go to any tabs website (where they have arrangements of songs for the guitar) and in about five minutes learn to play some of the top Beatles songs. It could take more effort and time to decide whether to buy the new Britney Whoever or Hilary Icouldnt-careless CD than to learn how to play some of your favorite pop songs. And once you have a few songs down, you'll be writing your own in no time. Then, lo and behold, your best friend will reveal that she has always wanted to play drums and—voilà!—you'll have a band.

What You'll Need

✓ instruments
✓ rehearsal space
✓ performance space
✓ microphone
✓ computer
✓ merch (T-shirts, stickers, paper, printer, computer design program)

"Music is a form of expression, and you can put into your music what it is hard to say in conversations. And that energy you get when you perform is like no other feeling in the world. It is truly amazing."

—Una Rose, 13, singer/guitarist for Blübird

RESOURCES

www.girlsrockcamp.org
Look here for info on this Portland-based rock camp, locations of other rock camps that might be near you, and more inspiring information.

www.azchords.com
A thorough website with guitar tabs and chords for just about every song in existence.

www.audacity.sorceforge.net
Free editing software.

www.apple.com
Go to this site to download GarageBand, a free editing software program.

www.cafepress.com
An excellent, easy-to-use website where you can make and sell your merch online.

✳ First Things First:
What to Play

OK, so you're feeling the power within you, the need to kick out the jams. But then it dawns on you—"I don't know how to play any instruments!" No problem.

Sid Vicious learned bass after he joined the Sex Pistols. The Donnas, an all-girl rock group that emerged in the '90s, organized their band when they were in eighth grade and taught themselves how to play as they went along. You don't need to already know how to play—but you do need to choose an instrument. Choose the one that most appeals to you, and choose it for the right reasons. For instance, don't pick bass because it seems easier or opt to be a vocalist because some people think girls shouldn't be drummers. **A musician's relationship with her instrument is an intimate and powerful one, and you'll never be happy in a band if you aren't playing an instrument that sings to you.**

Not sure where to start? Well, how about trying out an instrument to see what it sounds and feels like. Go to your local music store and ask if you can test the drums or strum a guitar. Don't get intimidated by male clerks who may assume that you don't know what you're doing. Bring a friend along for support, and assert your right to rock out! And don't let your outside appearance define what you play—you might be the shyest and gentlest girl in school, but that doesn't mean you can't thrash on a drum kit with the best of them.

If you don't want basic rock/pop instruments—like guitar, bass, drums, keyboard, or vocals—pick something alternative, such as adding distortion to the flute you play for the school band or programming beats on your computer. JD of Le Tigre programs much of the band's music, and Mona of Raining Jane will often play a wooden box and other interesting percussion. Most important is that you play what you like and you like what you play.

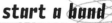
Gathering the Troops:
Who's on Drums?

The word *band* obviously implies more than just, well, you. So if you want to start a band, you have to be something of an organizer, as well as a musician.

Here are some ways to get started:

1. Simply ask musicians you know if they want to be in your band.

2. Approach the school band, especially if you need a drummer (often the hardest role to fill).

3. Post a sign at your school listing what roles your band has yet to fill.

4. Post an ad on a site like MySpace or Facebook.

You can also hold auditions. Since listening to someone play by themselves won't necessarily tell you if they'd fit into your band, pick an easy song and play it with them to see if there's chemistry. It's also essential that you talk thoroughly about music styles and interests to make sure it's a good match.

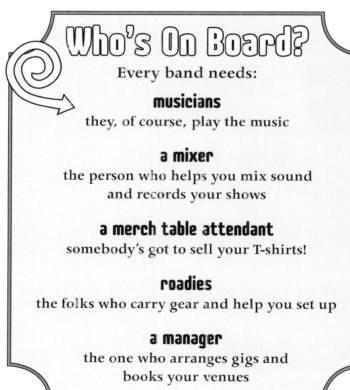

Who's On Board?

Every band needs:

musicians
they, of course, play the music

a mixer
the person who helps you mix sound and records your shows

a merch table attendant
somebody's got to sell your T-shirts!

roadies
the folks who carry gear and help you set up

a manager
the one who arranges gigs and books your venues

It's vital that you form a band with people you feel comfortable with. Trying out new songs and sharing what you've written can be nerve-wracking, and the last thing you want is to be surrounded by people who mock you or ignore your opinions. It doesn't matter how good a guitarist someone is or if they have the makings of a great rehearsal room in their basement — **you'll be happier playing kazoos in a dusty field with band members who respect you.** And keep it girls-only if it makes you and your bandmates more comfortable. Boys can be a great addition to a band, but they can sometimes unintentionally make female musicians feel self-conscious or insecure.

"I have learned that in order to be in a band with someone you have to like each other. That's pretty obvious. You also have to be able to listen to other people's ideas and be flexible while staying true to your own ideas. This is valuable when you write songs because you don't want to ignore other people and start a conflict."

—**Una Rose**, 13, singer/guitarist for Blübird

Leader of the Pack:
How to Keep the Peace When You Play

It will be a miracle if you never have a clash of egos in your band. But, as the band leader, you need to know how to deal with hurt feelings, anger, and differences of opinion.

There are lots of ways to work out typical band problems.

1 · Compromise. This is a great way to not only end a conflict but also produce great music. You may have the perfect vision for your band and a hundred great songs already written when out of the blue your guitarist decides she wants to write songs, too. **Instead of fighting her on it, work with her — the band**

may even end up being better for it. Everyone knew John and Paul were the songwriting geniuses behind the Beatles, but if they hadn't recorded songs that George wrote, we'd never have "While My Guitar Gently Weeps."

2. Take a break. Rehearsals can be grueling. If there's tension in the air, recommend that everyone take a walk around the block. Sometimes people get grumpy just because they're physically uncomfortable from standing or sitting or playing too long.

3. Ask your parents to mediate. They are less emotionally involved and can bring some objective perspective to the table.

Getting Started:
We're a Band—Now What?

So you have your girls, a great band name, and awesome outfits to wear at your first, TBA gig. And there you are, at your first rehearsal, staring at one another and picking your noses. How do you start? At a first band rehearsal, there are two very important things you should do.

Throw Around Some Ideas

Talk about what kind of music you want to create. It's OK if there are different ideas—most bands are made better by the members' varying interests. But make sure you are basically on the same page, so one girl doesn't think she's in a death metal band while another thinks she going to be singing backup vocals in a new age jazz group.

Play!!!

There's nothing worse for a new band than endlessly sitting around and talking about stuff. Band members can get into arguments and break up before a single note has been played. Making music together is a form of communication unlike anything else. So, just start. Play a couple of chords. If only one of you knows how to play an instrument, the others can begin by just singing along to the music. Or write a poem together and then speak it over a beat. You can only make music if you can get started.

> *"Try to hear everyone's ideas and see how you can complement the sounds being created. The more you really listen to each other, the more productive your band practices will be and the tighter you will sound."*
>
> —**Mona Tavakoli**, drummer for Raining Jane

♠ Tricks of the Trade:
If You Like the Music, You'll Love the Shirt!

A band just isn't a band without its music—or its merch! *Merch* is music biz lingo for merchandise, which can be CDs, T-shirts, stickers, posters, coffee mugs, mouse pads, cupcakes, or anything at all, as long as it's emblazoned with your band's logo. Don't underestimate the sheer coolness of leaning into the microphone and telling a crowd of hundreds, "Check out our merch table." It's like saying, "Hey, we're for real!" And making good merch doesn't have to be expensive or difficult. Try the following suggestions for starters.

The All-Important Demo

As soon as you can manage it, make a demo CD. Even if you record just one or two songs, people who like your sound will want it. Print your logo right on the disc or draw cool images onto it using colored Sharpies. **The main thing is to start spreading your sound.** Getting a demo together is pretty easy—check out the Insider Tips on the next page to see how it's done.

INSIDER TIPS
How to Make a Great Demo

As a new band, your demo is not only great merch but also a link to getting gigs, so it's important to do it right. Here are three ways.

1. The easiest way to record a demo is to **use your computer.** Almost any computer can record music, through either a built-in microphone or an external mic that you plug into a mini-jack. You'll probably need an adapter from the local electronics store that can interface between the mic chord and the computer. There are lots of low-cost and even free programs you can use to record music. If you have a Mac, GarageBand may come with your computer. Another good program that works with both PCs and Macs is Audacity, and you can download that online for free.

2. An alternative to your computer, especially if you want to record at a concert, is a **portable music player** (such as the iRiver or Minidisc players) that can record audio. Go to a local electronics store and ask an employee which are the best of the least-expensive ones. Once you record onto the portable device, you can easily move these files to your computer, where you can then clean the tracks up with Audacity or GarageBand's editing tools.

3. You can also go old school and **record to a cassette recorder,** but then you're forever limited to copying to cassette, rather than CDs, unless you have a special device that can record directly to CDs.

Whichever way you record, do lots of tests to make sure you have the right sound levels. Because of the volume they produce, drums are especially difficult to capture and can come out as loud crunchy sounds if not carefully recorded. To minimize distortion, you may need to put the microphone all the way across the room.

If you're up for recording live, many venues will allow you to record off the soundboard, and you'll probably get better sound than you would achieve at home. Just hand them your recorder and the right cables (usually XLR adaptors of some sort). The only downside is that there are no do-overs!

In addition to having a demo, make sure your band has a MySpace page where you can post new songs and send people to listen to them.

Wear It on Your Sleeve

Everyone has the ability to make band T-shirts. First, buy some cheap T-shirts. To make your logo, grab a cool image from the web, a digital photo you've taken, or something you drew on the computer. Incorporate your band logo using software like Photoshop or Gimp (a free open source program), and transfer the design onto printer iron-ons (sheets of printer paper made especially to iron on to clothing). Before printing, use either your graphics program or the software that came with the iron-ons to reverse the image, because you'll be ironing the image on backwards.

If you don't want to go the computer route, buy fabric paints at the art store and make a bunch of customized shirts. For these, create a stencil of your band logo with cardboard or stiff paper and paint through that. Check out the Fashion Company section (on page 96) for more detailed instructions on making T-shirts.

Stuck on You

Stickers are a very popular and cheap way to get your band known. Buy some sticker paper for your printer, and print smaller versions of that cool design you made for your T-shirt onto a bunch of stickers. Or make your own sticker designs by hand—just be sure to use permanent and waterproof paints and markers.

Flying High

Flyers to promote your gigs are a necessity, but they could turn into art pieces unto themselves. If you've come up with cool designs and original artwork, try selling them at your merch table as a memento of a gig after it's passed. Most of the great punk rock flyers were collages of images that made some kind of social commentary, and they ended up selling in galleries years afterward.

Out of the Box

Fuzzy key chains? Baseball caps? Branded Band-Aids? Make whatever you like and whatever you think will sell—the more people who buy your merch, the more publicity (and pocket change) you'll rake in.

Lights, Camera, Action!
Getting Gigs

When you have some songs down and are ready for an audience, playing a gig can be as simple as inviting a bunch of friends to your house for a show. But if you'd like to get a little more pro about it, there are lots of places to play outside of 21-and-over bars. You'll open up your options even more if you and your bandmates invest in a generator, a small motor that makes electricity when fed some gasoline. With a generator, you can play pretty much anywhere.

For gig ideas, try:

School

School talent shows and assemblies are great venues at which to play for your peers. You'll have to arrange this with the administration, so find out who takes care of this sort of thing at your school. Also, many schools host special fairs or carnivals. Ask your principal if you can set up a band area where you can rock out for the day.

Outdoor Venues

Unless you're playing an acoustic set (just instruments and no amplification), you'll need that generator for most of these. Try the bandstand at your local park or the middle of an abandoned lot. Some open spaces require sound permits so check with your local parks and recreation office. Your grandma's ranch or even your own backyard might be perfect, but be mindful of any neighbors within earshot of the noise.

Indoor Stages

If you start feeling confident and have a couple of gigs under your belt, consider an all-ages venue—there are usually a few in most towns that will welcome a fresh face on their stage. Don't be shy about asking for an audition or handing over a demo.

INSIDER TIPS
Finding Rehearsal Space

For many bands, the hardest obstacle can be finding a place to rehearse. Here are some ideas.

Home

If you have a drummer, pick her house. It's a lot easier to transport guitars than a drum kit. Of course, it's safe to assume that no parent will want band practice at their house *every* weekend. Each band member should talk to her parents about their schedules. Is there a convenient time for THEM? A time every weekend when they'll be out shopping or meeting friends and won't be in the house? You could even play it like they could have a "vacation" from parenting during your rehearsals and promise you'll stay safe and indoors, just jamming.

Community Centers

Most neighborhoods have a community center or Boys and Girls Club. See if there is a spare room in which you guys could bang around for an hour or two each week. Many community music centers will also have rehearsal space for a low fee (your folks might chip in if they feel it will spare their eardrums).

School

Schools will often give up classrooms to various extracurricular clubs. Try starting up a club called Our Rock Band, and see if you can get a classroom for a weekly rehearsal.

Camp

Rock schools and camps for girls have become a new trend that is spreading rapidly. You can find these in Portland, New York, Chicago, Philadelphia, and many other cities, and many of them also create afterschool programs that include band coaching and rehearsal space. Check *www.girlsrockcamp.org* to see if there's one in your area.

¢ Selling Out Without Selling Out:
How to Raise Funds

If you are starting a band, you are most likely doing it for the love of playing music. And that's good because, despite the few rock bands that eventually make it big, most bands work hard for little pay. Still, all musicians need to eat (and to buy new amps or extra drumsticks from time to time), so it's important to know how to raise a few bucks.

When you're starting out it can be tough to ask people to pay very much for your shows. You can, however, remind them (from stage, in between songs) to purchase some merch or tell them that there is a jar on your merch table for donations. You can also look for gigs at weddings or parties, where you might get a flat fee. **And don't be afraid of the time-honored tradition of** *busking,* **or playing on the streets.** Many great bands started that way—the old-time rock band Rube Waddell used to play every week in front of the same shoe store at the same time, and its weekly free show became a big hit. With a guitar case open for coins and bills, the change piles up fast. And you'll get a large and diverse audience to boot!

"The hardest thing I've experienced in a band is being open to criticism from other band members. Expressing yourself and opening up about ideas—lyrics, melodies, grooves—makes you vulnerable, but you have to trust that everyone wants what is best for the group and that their feedback aims to better whatever it is you're working on."

—**Mona Tavakoli**, drummer for Raining Jane

2 publish a ZINE

"**I could see that I was making a difference in people's lives,** and that is what kept me going through the very darkest of times —and there were many dark times. Many *ROCKRGRL* readers have gone on to have brilliant careers in music. That has been very rewarding. We published some of the first cover stories ever with Sleater-Kinney and the Donnas."

—**Carla DeSantis**, former publisher of *ROCKRGRL* magazine

Get It in Writing

Although people spend a lot of time reading on the Internet, no computer interface can imitate the pleasure of curling up on the couch with a favorite magazine or book. And even though it seems like some so-called expert is always talking nonsense about how young people don't read anymore, you know it's not true. Big books like the ones in the Harry Potter series have sold millions, magazines like *Seventeen* continue to take up prime shelf space in book stores, and teens are reading (and making!) indie publications like zines.

The word *zine* is short for magazine or fanzine, and it generally describes an independent (meaning people publish it on their own) magazine. **Zines can be glossy or photocopied, political or hilarious, and written by just about anyone.** These independent publications have a history that stretches as far back as the 1930s, though the modern idea of the zine was shaped mainly by the folded-over, half-sized zines of the 1970s—'90s punk movement. Zines today come in all sizes and forms.

And while computers have made it shockingly easy to publish a professional-looking book or magazine, there's also a great deal to be said in favor of using cut-and-paste methods, typewriters, and other ancient tools of the trade. If you want, you could even spend a year creating just one copy of one zine and treat it as an art object rather than as a mass-produced piece of literature (though that might not be the best way to get your voice out there). The point is, all that's standing between you and being a published writer, graphic artist, or magazine editor is a little bit of know-how and a lot of energy.

So if you are a writer or artist and love books, magazines, comics, and anything else with pages, it's time to get started on your own zine. There are literally millions of readers out there just like you, looking for something to inspire their imagination.

What You'll Need

- ✓ scissors
- ✓ glue stick
- ✓ paper
- ✓ art supplies (markers, colored pencils)
- ✓ copy machine
- ✓ computer (optional)
- ✓ page layout software (optional)

"Always stay true to yourself, your style. Without passion you cannot get very far. Your readers can see through empty work. They want to make sure YOU love the content as much as they do."

— **Ashley Qualls, 17, graphic designer and creator of Whaterlife Inc. & Whaterlife Magazine, LLC** (*www.whaterlife.com*)

RESOURCES

Scribus
Free desktop publishing software that can help you lay out your pages and create your whole zine. *www.scribus.com*

Nvu
Free web design software for building an online version of your zine without needing to know much html. *www.nvu.com*

Zine Book
Comprehensive zine info site with links to things like stores, other zines, and helpful how-tos. *www.zinebook.com*

www.zinester.com
Website that allows you to send out newsletters and establish mailing lists.

Stolen Sharpie Revolution: A DIY Zine Resource
by Alex Wrekk
A comprehensive book on how to make zines.

First Things First:
What Kind of Zine?

The first thing you have to do is decide on your zine's focus. Every zine has its own culture (sometimes it's more like a cult!), and many are written about the strangest subjects. Unlike larger magazines, zines tend to attract fans by being really specific about what they cover. Just look at the zine called *Dishwasher*. The creator, Peter Jordan, was this guy who made a goal to wash dishes in every one of the 50 states. He started his zine to document his journey. It may sound absurd, but his tales about all the interesting people he met while traveling were actually funny and even poignant. Another zine called *Found* published only things the editor found on the street, like letters, photos, and other stuff people left lying around. **The best zines follow a peculiar or obsessive interest of the publisher (that's YOU, if it's your zine) and catch the imagination of people with similar obsessions.** Because they don't have gigantic ad budgets (or any budget at all) they have to tap into communities and catch people's interest on the newsstand. Which zine are you more likely to pick up, one called *Animals* or another called *Rodents and the People Who Love Them*?

the zine

for girls

with

snap

So, don't waste time worrying about who will be interested in reading your ramblings about the backlash of 11th-grade postmodern feminist politics.

If you do the zine well, and really dig deep into the issue, it's pretty much guaranteed you'll find an audience. Even if it's only 15 people, that's more than you've got now, right?

You *will* have to worry about some logistical things: How often will your zine come out? What size will it be? Though you may want to put out a new edition every week, it's best to have more reasonable expectations regarding time and organization. Start by doing a quarterly, which means publishing every three months. That gives you plenty of time to kick your slacker friends into gear. Of course, you don't have to decide on a regular schedule at all, but it can help build your readership if you do.

Gathering the Troops:
Who's Got Something to Say?

With homework and everything else in your life, publishing a zine alone could be difficult, so it helps if you have people to help. Workload aside, it's also just more fun to work on a magazine with your pals.

As the editor in chief, you'll have to recruit a staff of writers, editors, and artists. To start, do a quick survey of your friends' talents. Do you have any writer friends who can churn out engaging prose (or even book reports) on a deadline? Do you know an illustrator or photographer who is just itching to see her work in print? You can also make decisions about the content of your zine depending on who gets involved. For instance, if you have a lot of artist friends, perhaps a comic anthology would be best. Your life will be easier if you adapt your zine to the talent you have available.

A staff can also help brainstorm ideas for the overall direction of the zine. Unlike the lucky few who've had one dream of one magazine all their lives, most of us have many ideas, and having a group of friends to discuss them with can make this process less paralyzing, especially if you create an atmosphere of trust and enthusiasm. When brainstorming ideas for your zine, ask everyone to talk about the magazines they all like, and toy with cool combinations of these publications (*Cosmogirl* meets *Popular Mechanic*, for instance) that could result in a great new zine.

It could also be cool to put out a publication that relates directly to girls and women, like *CineChick* (spotlighting women in cinema) or *Shutter Girl* (about teenage girl photographers). That could mean an all-female staff, though lots of girl-driven magazines like *Ms.* or *Bust* are happy to employ men, as long as they seem to be in support of and into the subject matter (meaning they won't try to turn *CineChick* into a zine about the prettiest female stars or insist that *Shutter Girl* is incomplete without a brother zine called *Shutter Guy*).

Who's On Board?

Every zine needs:

editor in chief

the person who oversees the whole zine and edits the stories

department editors

they oversee certain sections, like Movies, Music, or Dishwashing, and edit the stories that come in to those sections

graphic designer

she combines text and images to make each page both beautiful and readable

writers, artists, and photographers

the geniuses who provide you with great stories and visuals for the zine

copy editor

the most detail-oriented girl, who checks for grammar problems, mistakes, and typos

Leader of the Pack:
Please Write Just One Page?

A lot of zine starters quickly get frustrated when their contributors don't take the project as seriously as they do. When your friends get things in late—or not at all!—tensions can definitely develop. But don't give up hope if your buddies show a lack of discipline. One main role of a good publisher or editor, even at the very highest levels, is to know how to cajole and coax her contributors into doing good work. These strategies will help get the best out of even the biggest procrastinators.

Set Deadlines

You may not care exactly when the zine is done, but your contributors don't need to know that. **There isn't an artist or writer alive who doesn't operate better with a deadline.** Many will wait until two hours before an article is due, then write something brilliant just in the nick of time! You can always push back a deadline as a special concession, but, as a rule, strict due dates are the way to go.

Be Enthusiastic and Encouraging

Artists need to know they're appreciated. You can ignite creative energy simply by reminding someone that she's an amazing illustrator, or that you can't wait to read the story she's writing about her grandmother's red shoes.

Gently Pester

Before the deadline hits, ask how the illustration or story is coming along. Don't be melodramatic about it (no one wants to write for an editor who is a drama queen), but do build a dialogue about the process before you're in crisis mode, as in: "I need your story ... yesterday!"

Move On

If someone is really dragging her feet, it's best to just produce the zine without her. It sucks to have to set a cohort free, but sometimes it's just not worth the energy to make someone do something they obviously can't or don't want to do. When you have to cut a friend's contribution from the magazine, do it with professionalism, and DO NOT let it ruin the friendship. If your zine starts getting readers and attention, she may come back to you with a better attitude. If the item in question is something important (like an illustration for the cover), start looking for backup solutions. In general, it's always good to have extra contributors in reserve, and be ready to pinch hit yourself.

When stories do finally come in and it's time to edit them, be gentle with your edits and requests for rewrites. It is one thing for an editor to demand a massive overhaul of an article from a paid writer, but very different to do so from an unpaid friend. Remember that zines tend to have an edgier feel about them than professional magazines, and don't harp on perfectionism.

Getting Started:
The Glue Stick Is Mightier Than the Sword

Before you get wrapped up in the exciting business of actually producing your zine, make an outline of how you want to arrange everything inside. Most magazines are divided into sections like Opinion, Features, Reviews, Hot Tips, etc. You, of course, can designate whatever sections you want (Cow-Watching Stories, Cows in the News, Cow Farm Directory), but do make sure there is logic and consistency to your layout and that it is reader-friendly. Think about your favorite magazines and how, right away, you always know where to find what you're looking for, then apply that strategy to your zine.

Once you have a basic outline, it's time to get your hands dirty. Here are three approaches to making a zine.

1·Handmade. People who do low-budget, alternative-minded zines are already going against the tide of technology and popular wisdom, so many of them disdain the use of computers for laying out a publication. They opt for low-tech (or no-tech) simplicity, using supplies like glue, staplers, and felt-tipped pens (see the next page). This is the true "indie" way of making a zine.

2·Higher tech. Of course, a computer can produce really cool stuff. The same type of software used by most major publications is totally available to you online. Programs like QuarkXPress (*www.quark.com*), Photoshop CS3, and InDesign CS3 (*www.adobe.com*) can be used for most publishing needs. They are not free, but their prices are usually discounted for students. Another option is a free, open source program, called Scribus, that you can download off the Internet. It helps with most of the same tasks (laying out pages, arranging images) as the pricey graphic design programs. (See page 32 for Digital Distribution tips.)

3·Hybrid. Even if you go the higher tech route, you still have to copy and staple your zine by hand, so it won't ever look completely polished. Embrace this mix-and-match sensibility by intentionally doing a hybrid approach—do the basic text layout and graphics with your computer, but leave space for drawings and other handmade additions.

♠ Tricks of the Trade:
Making a DIY Zine

Even if you do use your computer for some aspects of production, be ready to assemble your zine by hand. **There's something special about the feel of a handmade zine.** Zines had their origins in the punk culture of the '70s—'90s; they were part of a cut-and-paste revolution often called DIY, which stands for "do it yourself." Punk bands and artists decided not to pay for 10 years of music lessons or wait for some record label or publisher to allow them to be heard by the world, and did literally everything by themselves—even making instruments and stapling together their clothes. This idea still permeates a lot of zine culture, and your courage and endurance for the often meticulous and even tedious work of cutting and pasting will earn you admirers.

To take this no-frills approach, you'll need some basic white letter-sized paper, your text and your images, markers and pens, scissors, tape or glue, a stapler, and a way to make copies. Follow these steps.

1. Count and fold. Decide how many pages you want your zine to be, then take half as many pieces of paper and fold them in half.

2. Write and draw. Unfold the zine and place your content on the newly created "pages." Write out the articles by hand with pens or markers, or print them out and paste them on the pages. Same with the art: Create it from scratch or paste it in. Use glue sticks and tape to put your zine together, adding assorted images, magazine cutouts, and whatever else you find.

3. Copy. After you have put all of your content and illustrations on each page, make copies of the whole zine (be sure to keep pages in order!).

4. Staple. Reassemble each zine and refold, stapling at the fold. Make sure you have a good, strong stapler, and attach the pages from the outside so the pointy tips will be buried in your zine.

INSIDER TIPS
Digital Distribution

Whether your zine is generated with a computer, your hands, or both, you can also distribute it in its full color (or black and white) glory on the web. Here are three ways to do that.

Generate a PDF

Most folks are familiar with PDFs, a type of file that is used for multipage documents with graphics. (If you go to a company's website and download its brochure, it's likely to be a PDF.) PDFs are great because they can contain cool text and graphics, but they use very little memory—that means they don't take up much space on a hard drive and are easy to send via email. Here's how to make a PDF of your zine. (If you've generated your zine using a program like Quark or Scribus, skip to Step 3.)

1 · Scan. Scan each page of your zine using Photoshop or other graphics software, and save each page as an individual file. If you don't have a scanner, try a big copy shop—most have a scanner you can use. Remember that each page, when scanned, becomes a picture, not a Word document. After it is scanned, you can move the whole picture, but not edit the text.

2 · Insert files. Take each one of those page files and insert it into a page layout tool like Scribus or into a word processing program like Microsoft Word (just select Insert, then Picture, then From File). Insert all of the files. If you are using a layout tool, the pages will face each other so it will look like a professional magazine; if you are using Word, each page will simply come after the next in one long document.

3 · Save as PDF. Now that you have your newly built electronic zine (or the one that you already made on the computer), select Print. You're not actually going to print it, but when the printing dialog box comes up, you'll click on the button that says PDF or Save As or Export. If you see another menu after that, choose the PDF option. Eventually, you'll be prompted to save, and voilà, a PDF will be made! Some programs, like InDesign, actually have an option in the menu that's just Export PDF. Once you have a PDF, you can email it to all of your fans, or post it as a link on your MySpace page, website, or blog.

Create a Website

With a little bit of html learning, or by using a free web design program like iWeb for the Mac or Nvu for all computers, you can put a page up that represents your zine. Because web links can mimic the process of turning pages, you can even make your website look zine-like.

To do this, though, you'll have to type the whole zine into the program (unless you initially created it on the computer and already have a copy on file). Scanned images of text won't work for a website because they will take way too long to upload. You'll still need to scan in the photos and art, though. As you are inputting all of the content, try to imitate the look of the zine, making the home page of the website look just like the front page of your zine. Then, make each page a truly separate page on the website, with a link to the next page and the previous page, so readers can experience each page individually and be able to read ahead or flip back.

Send Out an html Newsletter

There are several services on the web, like *www.zinester.com*, that allow you to send out newsletters, or e-zines, in html form (if you know how to write in html), so you can design them with the same sort of visual flair found in your zines. These services also have a program that sets up a newsletter mailing list for you. To get people on your mailing list, you can either collect their addresses or put a link on your website where they can sign up.

> *"If you believe in what you're doing and what you want, you can have it. Never give up. Although it's competitive out there and it may seem too hard to keep up, you CAN do it."*
>
> —**Ashley Qualls**, 17, graphic designer and creator of Whaterlife Inc. & Whaterlife Magazine, LLC (*www.whaterlife.com*)

Lights, Camera, Action!
Getting People to Read Your Stuff

The most important thing about making a zine is attracting as many readers as possible. To do that, you need to make lots of copies. Ask your mom or dad if they can make some copies at their offices (offering to pay for the paper), or hit up friends who work at copy stores to help get you good deals on large orders (always ask for student rates). Copies can get expensive: Be prepared to spend your allowance and other cash earned from part-time jobs to get your new endeavor under way.

There are more ways than you might think to get your zine read. You can leave stacks at cafés, hand them out at school during lunch, or host a release party during which you give away free copies. While it may be difficult to get your zine into large stores, most local independent bookstores will be happy to carry a copy or two.

Another great way to get attention for your zine is to create a presence on the web. Even the most homegrown zinesters know that technology isn't *all* bad. Set up a website, or at the very least a Facebook or MySpace page, and network with folks who have similar ideas or feelings about the world. Include on your site how people can order copies. If your zine is about getting corn stuck in one's teeth, do a search on the web for corn and teeth—you'll likely find at least one site dedicated to those who valiantly struggle with toothpick in hand. Offer to send a sample copy. There are also countless zine sites where you can meet fellow zinesters—and they'll turn out to be your most avid readers.

¢ Selling Out Without Selling Out:
How to Raise Funds

Making a zine is about getting read, not making bank. Don't expect to make a profit producing a zine—it's really a labor of love. Even larger independent magazines struggle to make money. This is not to say that you can't find ways to support your zine financially. Try these suggestions.

1· Organize your band friends to perform at a benefit concert.

2· Include several slam poets in your latest issue and host a paid-admission poetry slam as part of your release party.

3· Do research at your local library for organizations that support independent arts and might give you a small grant.

4· Ask your friends who have bands, or perform in other ways, if you can sell copies at their shows.

5· Set up a table outside the local café and sell copies there. The most important thing is to gather enough pennies to keep your zine going.

"Personally, I find it somewhat hard being a teenage girl and balancing my time between friends and work. When you dedicate yourself to publishing something—whether it be a book, website, or what have you—it can take a lot of your energy and dedication. It also takes a lot of strength to maintain the balance of friends you want and need. Try not to dedicate 110 percent of your time to what you're working on. And have FUN with what you're doing. Heck, even invite your friends in to watch and help! I did!"

—**Ashley Qualls**, 17, graphic designer and creator of Whaterlife Inc. & Whaterlife Magazine, LLC (*www.whaterlife.com*)

3 put on a PLAY

Born for the Stage

Most kids, at some point, have made their parents sit through a re-creation of *Charlotte's Web* that featured a stuffed animal as the pig and a web made from toilet paper and glue; or perhaps it was a puppet show starring a prince and a princess, an evil monster, and a cow jumping over a moon. Though you might cringe when looking back on your childhood theatrics, those amateur endeavors still constituted real live theater—one of the most exciting, impulsive, and emotional art forms on the planet. Plays have been around since the Greeks started slinging the first written words on stage several thousand years ago, and the art form has continued to be an integral part of our society.

Theater can be anything, from a means of entertainment to political commentary to a historical documentary. It represents the voice of the people and has always been a great impetus for massive gatherings of villagers, community members, and friends alike.

Though film and TV have become the modern world's most popular avenues for storytelling, theater has a unique and exciting energy that keeps it thriving in our culture. Because it's always live, it has more intensity, and the same play is always a little different each time you see it. And making theater is a different experience than making film. The focus in theater is on the big picture, as opposed to the narrow camera shot, so all the actors, even when they aren't speaking, are still involved in the action. Body language and vocal projection mean more in theater because actors' faces are not always easy to see, nor their voices heard, from far out in the audience.

And you don't need to act to be in a play. Are you a good observer and leader? Be the director. Love to tell stories? Write a play. Not so good at words but love pictures? Design a set. There's a niche for just about every kind of personality in the theater.

What You'll Need

- ✓ a play
- ✓ a stage
- ✓ an audience
- ✓ actors
- ✓ costumes
- ✓ sound equipment (optional)

Shakespeare's
HAMLET
1603

"The most important thing that I've learned about doing theater is that it is about the whole company, not just the main leads. Just because you have been assigned a part that's not so fabulous, doesn't mean that YOU are not fantastic. Every role counts—every word spoken, every action, every emotion plays a huge part in a production."

— **Angela Chen, 16, actress**

RESOURCES

www.creativedrama.com
A website chock-full of scripts, theater games, and other inspirations.

www.childdrama.com
Despite the kiddie-like name, this is a good resource for budding theater folks of any age.

✷ First Things First: Choosing a Style

The great thing about theater is that it really can be whatever you want it to be. Unlike a book, which has to include words people understand, a play could be in gibberish. Unlike dance, a play doesn't have to involve movement. If you look at any three random plays, like Shakespeare's romantic comedy *A Midsummer Night's Dream*, Suzan-Lori Parks' dark tragedy *Top Dog, Underdog*, and director Julie Taymor's innovative production of *The Lion King*, it's easy to see that theater can be anything. The possibilities are literally endless.

Here is a sampling of basic theater styles, but feel free to combine them to make up your own.

Tragedy

Bad things happen—and then they get worse. Tragedies often help us to understand important things about human nature. For instance, Margaret Edson's *Wit* is about a hardened professor of literature who, while dying of cancer, learns valuable life lessons about humility and love.

♥

Comedy

Something bad may happen, and probably will, but the ending is happy. Sometimes comedies are laugh-out-loud funny, and other times they are just stories where all of the problems are resolved and everything turns out for the best, from a musical like *Hairspray* (in which Tracy Turnblad and her friends continue to get rejected by a fat-phobic and racist TV dance show until they fight back and earn their place in pop culture) to Neil Simon's play *The Odd Couple* (in which a slob and a neat freak somehow learn to live together).

Tragi-Comedy

This is a mixture of the first two styles—a somewhat sad story that ends happily, or a happy/funny story that ends badly. Shakespeare's *A Winter's Tale* is a good example of the first. It starts out with a jealous king calling for the execution of his wife, and it ends with her being rescued and everyone living happily ever after. Tragi-comedies can

also finish on a question mark, without a clear happy or sad ending. This type of play can also be classified as a black comedy, or a comedy with dark themes.

Satire

The main goal of satire is to poke fun at powerful organizations or people as a way to make a critique or point out how things could be better. Christopher Durang is a popular playwright who does this well by taking truthful aspects of people and institutions and exaggerating them until they are funny and even grotesque. In *Sister Mary Ignatius Explains It All for You*, he pokes fun at the strictness of nuns in Catholic school.

Musical Theater

This genre is just like it sounds—theater with song and dance. These plays can vary widely, from the 1950s-era poodle skirt and drag-racing fun of *Grease* to the more tragic tale of poverty and persecution during the time of the French revolution in *Les Miserables*. Got friends who sing? Get them involved!

Solo Shows

In recent years, the solo show has become popular. There is only one person on stage, sometimes telling a long story or playing many different characters in a play with several parts. Solo shows usually rely heavily on acting and story-telling and very little on sets and costumes. A few good examples (which were filmed and can be rented) are Spaulding Gray's *Swimming to Cambodia*, in which Gray talks about his experiences being an actor in the film *The Killing Fields,* and Anna Deavere Smith's *Fires in the Mirror*, which is about a deadly car accident in New York that provoked a lot of racial tension between two ethnic groups (Smith interviewed all of the people involved and then embodied them on stage).

Different styles (or "genres") of theater are demanding in different ways. **Comedy may seem easier because you don't have to get your lead actor to cry every night, but many people will tell you that comedy is more difficult because of the need for precise timing and delivery (it's hard to be funny!)** Musical theater, of course, requires singers and musicians, while satire requires a great sense of humor and timing. Decide what kind of a play you want to do based on your interests, which actors you can rally to the cause, and what kind of finances you have. See Getting Started on page 49 for more ideas on how to select or make your own play.

Gathering the Troops:
How to Hold Auditions

When most people think of putting on a play, the first thing that comes to mind is the dreaded audition. Truth is, there are lots of other people you'll need besides a cast. You'll need set and costume designers, builders, a stage manager, possibly a writer, and definitely people to run lights and sound. But, yes, you will also need actors.

You could just handpick people for roles, but it's highly recommended that you hold auditions. As dreaded as they are, auditions help prevent casting from becoming a popularity contest. Everyone will have a crack at the roles, and you may find yourself shocked at people's talent. The mega-cheerful popular girl may turn out to have depths of emotion you never expected, while the loner guy may be hilarious once on stage. Though actors may feel painfully rejected after an audition, they will at least know they gave it their best shot.

If you are the one holding auditions, follow these guidelines to make them go smoothly and to get the best results out of your actors.

Scheduling
Draw up an audition schedule and try to stick to it. It is a mess if everyone shows up at once. This will also give you the opportunity to see who is punctual (a very important quality in the theater biz) and who couldn't remember what day it was even if they had a calendar tattooed on their forearm.

Safety in Numbers
Ask one of the other folks working on the play to sit in on the auditions with you. They can help with the casting and defuse some of the hurt feelings if someone is upset after not getting the part they wanted.

Have Actors Prepare a Monologue
A monologue means "one person speaking," as opposed to a dialogue, which happens between more than one person. Most plays have at least one great monologue, or speech. For auditions, ask people to prepare a short monologue.

It could be something they have written themselves cr a few lines one character says in a movie. From hearing an actor read something they've prepared, you can get an idea of their body language and how they construe emotion without a script getting in the way.

Ask Actors to Cold Read

In addition to asking each actor to perform a monologue, prepare scenes from the play (called "sides" in an audition) for actors to read with each other. The point is to see how the actor embodies the character they are trying out for. (If the play is not written yet, have actors read scenes from another play in the same genre, just to see how they interact with others on stage.)

It's best to audition people in pairs because it will speed up the process, but if that's not possible, ask your casting assistant to read the scene with the actor. You can hand out the scenes to the actors as they arrive and give them a few minutes to practice while others have their auditions.

Decisions

Out of respect, let actors know promptly if they've landed a role or not. **People will be hurt when they are cut, but they will appreciate being notified.** If you can't decide on the first go-round, have callbacks, or a second round of auditions. The simplest way to notify people of being cast, cut, or called back is to post a list on a bulletin board. But if you have time, send kind personal emails. This is always appreciated, especially by those not cast this time around.

CALLBACKS
- M'shell
- Janet
- Yuki
- Stefanie
- Zoey

Leader of the Pack:
How to Direct Actors

You don't have to be the director to get a production going. For example, if you're a fashionista with a vision of a bunch of 19th-century ball gowns that you'd like to design, organize people to be in a play with your awesome costumes, then go back to working with cloth and ignore all the drama (so to speak).

But, regardless of your role, the show will need a director—and if you have a vision of the production, it may as well be you. Wondering if girls are as good at directing as guys? Yes! Sometimes even better! Girls have just as strong artistic visions, and, during teenage years, are typically more responsible (an important skill in directing). Twenty years ago, there were very few women directing plays, but that has shifted a lot over the years. Now, many women run major theater companies. So, if you want to direct the show, go for it. And don't feel tied to doing a girl-centered play about sisters or a feminist critique from the '60s—direct anything you want, any way you want. A play about male scientists throughout history? Sure. A play about a pro football team? Why not? As long as you have respect for your actors and for the play, it'll be great. Believe in yourself, and your crew will believe in you, too.

In a small production, a director may have many roles (lighting design, costume design, sound design, and even selling the cookies before the show), but her priority should be getting the best performances out of her actors. The director must create an imaginary world that the audience will believe in, and all of the great sets and costumes in the world won't draw people into your imaginary world if the actors don't believe the things they're saying.

The funny thing about acting is that it's hard to say what makes it really good—but we certainly know when it's bad! If you are the director, the single most important thing you can do is figure out what you consider good acting and help your performers to achieve that.

The most identifiable sign of talent is when an actor looks comfortable on stage. Nothing loses an audience faster than a fidgety actor, talking in an unnaturally squeaky voice, and hiding behind scenery. If your actors are comfortable, the audience will be too. Then, if they forget a line or laugh when they're supposed to be angry, the audience will just believe that's the way it's supposed to be. An actor who is natural and focused on the imaginary world you've created will convince audience members that they should be focused on it, too. The question is how you, as a director, can help actors get comfortable.

Lead, Don't Push

Actors respond much better when you ask them to use their own brains and hearts. So if you want an actor to cry in a scene, don't say "Cry! Now!" Very few people can do that on command anyway. A better approach would be to ask them about what their character is going through, and how they think that would feel. See if they can relate on some level.

And every actor needs to understand her motivation—what her character wants in a scene. In his book *Audition*, acting teacher Michael Shurtleff says that emoting for an actor should be like sweating for a runner: A runner doesn't command herself to sweat—she runs up hills and stays focused on her goals and the sweat comes naturally. In other words, an actor playing a character whose main drive is to complete high school should focus all of his energy on that. Then, when obstacles come up, like his car breaks down on the way to school, he won't need to be directed to "cry"—he'll just do it.

Playing Games

It may sound a little goofy, but playing some basic theater games can really help actors to stop overthinking things, overcome their fears, and better inhabit the world of their characters. To get you started, here are three games directors use.

1 · The Zoo. Have your actors sit around and decide what kind of animal their characters would be. Have them act out those animals, without words, in an improv. Then have them do their scenes, not as their characters, but as the animals they chose. And then, finally, run the scene normally.

2 · Voice Power. Have everyone play their parts blindfolded, so they rely only on voice, rather than body language, to communicate. The process will have them feeling less self-conscious about their bodies and more focused on the emotional quality of their voices.

3 · Character Field Trips. Have everyone go on a field trip to the nearest store to buy something, but stipulate that they must stay in character while on the street and in the store.

Improvisation (Improv)

Asking actors to create a scene without using a script will force them to see their characters as truly alive and not just as words on a page. Have actors either improvise scenes that happen outside of the play (to give them a better sense of their prior lives or of events that happen offstage) or play out scenes actually in the play but using their own words (this is especially helpful when performing Shakespearean plays or anything else with a difficult language).

play

Go Team!

There's nothing like getting everyone to feel as though they're on a real team. **Listen to people's ideas, and, even if you don't love them, try out the ideas to see if they work.** Also, have at least one party or get-together that's not a rehearsal and just an event held for people to laugh and get to know one another. You can also play fun games during or after rehearsal (like Twister or soccer) or just do anything that creates some bonding experiences. Acting takes a huge amount of trust. When you are on the stage, you can feel very vulnerable, and knowing that all the other actors have your back is incredibly reassuring.

> *"The greatest thing about acting is that you can be anyone or thing you want to be. It is also a great way to let your emotions out and feel a different side of your personality that you've never felt before. It has personally given me a chance to be an animal, a villain, a bar girl, and other various wacky characters."*
>
> —**Angela Chen**, 16, actress

INSIDER TIPS
Blocking

Blocking is the art of planning where actors will stand on stage. This is one of the crucial tasks of the director because the greatest theatrics in the world will go to waste if the audience can't see and hear your actors.

Rules of Thumb

1· You must ensure that actors never have their backs to the audience, stand in one place for too long without reason, or upstage (block the audience from seeing or hearing) another actor.

2· You can also use blocking to create interesting moments and tension. For instance, if there's a scene in which a kid is trying to tell her father that she never felt like they were friends, you could have the actors speak their lines from opposite sides of the stage to emphasize the emotional distance between the two characters.

3· If you want your play to have a realistic feel, make sure that you let the lines and the actors themselves guide the blocking, so that the scenes look natural. And don't over-block a scene or it may look chaotic or stiff. But if your play is meant to look very unrealistic (like some comedy sketches or absurdist pieces), then use more elaborate or stylized blocking to highlight the weirdness of the world of your play.

4· Hire a stage manager to write down the blocking and gently remind people where to go when they forget. These notes will also be useful for a director who's trying to work out new blocking for a scene. To know where to tell actors to go, you should know these spots on a stage.

upstage
This is the top of the stage, farthest from the audience.

downstage
This is the bottom of the stage, closest to the audience.

stage left
The left side of the stage from the perspective of the actors (also called house right).

stage right
The right side of the stage from the perspective of the actors (also called house left).

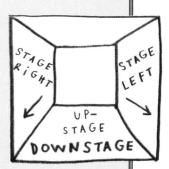

Who's On Board?

Every play needs:

director
she coaches the actors and shapes the whole production

actors
the people who play the characters

stage manager
she takes care of all the little details, like getting actors into their spots, keeping rehearsals on schedule, maintaining contact lists, and setting up the stage before a show

costume designer/builder
the person who gathers, and sometimes makes, the costumes

set designer/builder
the person who dreams up what the stage will look like and/or actually builds and/or buys the pieces that go on it

"The most important thing to me is to surround myself with enthusiastic, passionate people. Every time I go into a new show, I'm creating a new team. One bad egg can really spoil everything, so I am really careful about who I work with."

—**Lisa Steindler**, artistic director of Encore Theatre Company, San Francisco

Getting Started:
Everything But the Kitchen Sink

So, as you've probably figured out by now, putting together a production can start in zillions of ways. Here are some of them.

Select or Write a Play

Do you have a favorite play (or type of play) you've always wanted to perform? Or have you written a play and just need actors? Once you have your material, the next step is to get a cast together and begin rehearsing. This is still how the majority of shows get started.

Who Forgot to Hit Record?

Come up with an overall story for your play, then have actors improvise scenes from it. Videotape the proceedings (or just record the audio) and build a script from the results. As the director, you'll want to give the actors something to work with, like: "In this scene, we know the penguin has to convince the police that she's being followed. Let's play it out." Some of the greatest material can come from this type of rehearsal. Christopher Guest, the director for the films *Waiting for Guffman* and *Best in Show*, works this way to generate material.

From Page to Stage

There's a great theater group based in San Francisco called Word for Word, and they don't use scripts at all—they use books. One person reads the narration, while the others act out the scenes and speak all the dialogue. You could do something similar with your group. No need to memorize all those pesky lines—just read straight from the books and make them part of the show. If you're basing your show on a novel, you'll need to edit down the book to the most essential parts for time's sake; to start, it may be better to use short stories.

The Forgotten Episode

Pick a TV show you like and write an episode from the point of view of a less-important character. For instance, what's the daily life of the Flanders children in *The Simpsons*? There's a fun play called *Security* by Joshua Pollock that focuses on two security guards from *Star Trek* and what they think about amid all the mayhem going on around them.

Docu-Diva

If you would like to do a play based on a real event, you should read up on the Tectonic Theater Project, a theater company located in New York. When writing a docudrama (a mix between a documentary and a drama), the entire cast goes and interviews people who lived through the event they are dramatizing. Then the actors come back and write the play based on the people they met and the interviews they conducted, using the actual words of these real people. The company's most famous play is *The Laramie Project*, which is about a young gay man who was murdered in Laramie, a small town in Wyoming. The cast all temporarily relocated to this town after the murder to build the story. Of course, you can also make a play about something less catastrophic, like the marriage of two older folks at a senior home.

Mix CDs Gone Wild

Find an album you really like and use it as the basis for a musical. Lip-synch the words or, if your friends are all great singers, get the karaoke version and sing over the songs. You can also bring in a band, or use a CD for storyline inspiration. A lot of albums are concept albums and lend themselves especially well to theatrical productions. Green Day's *American Idiot*, for instance, could be the soundtrack for a political play about how the media has dumbed down the public. Other albums just have particularly storylike songs that would fit into a musical—Suzanne Vega's "Luka" is a good example. You can develop a character and storyline by using lyrics from the song ("My name is Luka/I live on the second floor...").

Tricks of the Trade:
Building Your Sets and Costumes

Sometimes just a few simple props can have great power. A pile of real dirt and a puddle of real water could go a long way toward setting a scene that takes place in a campground. Or what about an enormous tree branch? Use one to create a forest scene, and make it double as a coat-rack for interior scenes. Oftentimes, staying simpler is better, because then you ask the audience to use their imagination instead of imperfectly imitating reality.

And don't be afraid to get creative. A production of Shakespeare's *The Tempest* that was directed by William Peters at San Francisco State University had a big slide coming from offstage to the middle of the stage. Characters brought props in, but that slide was the only set piece. It became a ship, a magic passage, shelter in the rain, and many other things. Because the actors believed it was all of these things, the audience did, too. In an Oregon Shakespeare Festival production of Thomas Middleton's *The Revenger's Tragedy*, a big red ribbon would shoot from a wound when a character was stabbed, replacing the standard fake blood. **By the end of the play, the stage was covered in red ribbons, poetically illustrating the extreme amount of violence that had taken place.**

The same principle is true with costumes. You can gain a lot of clues about a character, and the places they live, by paying attention to their clothing; a shiny new top hat says something very different than a dirty old baseball cap. If you're doing a play from another time, like the Roman era, instead of trying to get everyone in togas, have all the Romans dress in contemporary black clothes and wear a single small strip of white fabric over their shoulders. It's not literal, but people will totally get it, and the use of metaphor in theater is unbelievably powerful.

And remember, for your first production, concentrate on the acting and the script and minimize sets and costume changes as much as possible. You want the focus to be on the performances, not the fake windows (that fall from rafters mid-production) or fancy costumes (that your actors don't have enough time to change into). Your audience would rather just see a good show that makes them feel something.

> "Gather the people you admire, trust, and have fun with, and start talking about what you want to build. If you want to win a Tony on Broadway, then start there, start building toward that goal. You don't need a penny to do it. Go to a park, a living room, get costumes from your parents or friends, and go do it."
>
> —**Lisa Steindler**, artistic director of Encore Theatre Company, San Francisco

Lights, Camera, Action!
Wherefore Art Thou, Oh Stage

So, you have your play, your cast, a directorial vision, and maybe even some costumes and set plans. But where are you going to have your show? Believe it or not, you don't actually need a theater. A play can be performed anywhere. The San Francisco Mime Troupe performs in parks all over Northern California. Playwright Wallace Shawn staged his play *The Fever* in various friends' apartments in New York.

Unique settings simply make for more interesting experiences. If you staged the musical *Grease* in your house, people could be led from room to room (or even outside) to see different scenes. Or you could write a play to fit a specific space—many cities have long-running murder mystery plays that unfold in spooky old houses. If you want a traditional stage, ask for permission to use the school auditorium or ask around at local theaters. If you perform at odd hours, a community theater company might be able to let you run your show when theirs isn't going on. Basically, don't let space be an obstacle. There isn't a kind of space on the planet that hasn't been used for theater.

¢ Selling Out Without Selling Out:
How to Raise Funds

P eople are used to theater being very expensive—most Broadway shows cost more than $100 a ticket now—so if you charge less than $10 for your performance, people will probably feel relieved. You can even make the tickets "sliding scale" (which means people pay based on how much they can afford, using the honor system). In this model, financially stable adults will pay more than students, which is only fair.

If you'd rather draw large crowds and not worry about tickets, there's a long tradition of passing a hat around after a show and merely accepting donations. There are theater companies in all of the major cities that make their whole living by "passing the hat."

> "The hardest thing about theater is having the strength and the determination to keep up with 110 percent of your performance, even though at times you might feel like giving up. Rehearsals run into the night, sometimes till midnight … I cannot tell you how many times I wanted to just crawl in a hole and sleep. But there was always work to be done, and it always paid off in the end."
>
> —**Angela Chen**, 16, actress

4 film a TV SHOW

Real World ... Really!

Ever notice that the stuff you see on TV is produced by people who don't know the first thing about what's really going on? They make it seem like the point of every girl's life is to act sexy (or dumb), know martial arts (or ballet), and have a super-cute boyfriend (or dog) all at once. Most TV shows are also just plain boring. How much do we need another reality show about vapid people trapped in a house together? Or a game show where everyone's quietest voice is a shriek?

Until recently, your only way to fight back against bad programming was to sit on the couch and throw things at the TV. Not anymore!
With some simple technology, you can create a TV show that has a real sense of humor and originality, and focuses on the things you actually care about—or at least find amusing.

Anyone who has used a cell phone to video their friends doing silly things has felt, in some small way, what it's like to make a television show. In fact, with a little effort and some basic knowledge, you could not only star in your own TV show about a secret agent who happens to be a talk show host and a neurosurgeon in her spare time, but you could also draw anywhere from three to a thousand viewers. And once you've mastered producing a TV show, you can move on to movies. The process is more complex, but the tools you need are the same. So why sit back and have unattainable fantasies shoved down your throat about the lives of people you couldn't care less about? Get out there and turn the river of imagery around—make the world watch what you're thinking about, rather than the other way around.

What You'll Need

✓ camera
✓ computer
✓ location
✓ USB/FireWire cable
✓ output device (program/DVD)
✓ headphones

"I love the fact that I can use this creative medium to tell a story and to state my opinions ... I'm so happy that I have found something that I am so passionate about and something that I want to keep with me for the rest of my life. Most people have relationships and significant others to keep themselves sane, I have video production. Without it, I'd go crazy."

—Emilie Collier, 19, filmmaker

RESOURCES

www.youtube.com
An amazingly varied, frustrating, and freeing place to upload your show to the world. (Turn off the Comments if you don't want to see the inevitable deluge of random—and sometimes offensive—remarks.)

www.reelgrrls.org
A group in Seattle that hosts intensive filmmaking camps for girls.

First Things First:
Sitcom or Reality Show?

Take a moment to think about who you are and what you want to achieve by making your own TV show—this will lead you to figuring out what type of program you want to produce. Have you been secretly studying kung fu and want to go all Jennifer Garner-style, punching your way to super-stardom? Or have you always seen yourself as an Oprah type, hugging everyone within an inch of their lives and making them cry on TV?

There are basically two kinds of TV shows: a scripted show (like a fictional drama or sitcom) and an unscripted show (a talk show, reality show, or news-based program). In general, scripted shows are much more time-intensive to make. Writing a script, memorizing lines, making sets for fictional locales, getting cameras in the right places for dramatic angles—all of that takes time and patience. If you're doing a scripted sitcom or drama series, you might start working on the story and gathering your crew in the spring, but you probably won't start shooting until summer. **An unscripted show can happen a lot faster: All you need is one location and a few interesting people to film.**

* A good way to ease into TV is to try an unscripted talk show. Start by coming up with a good idea. Do you have friends who are into the supernatural? Make a talk show about UFOs, astral projection, mind-reading, and ghosts. Invite your friends and other local enthusiasts on to talk about their beliefs and theories, and get footage of local spots where weird, creepy things have allegedly occurred.

Regardless of the type of show you choose, leave yourself enough time to do it right. No matter how simple and stupid things often look on TV, a lot of skill and time goes into creating that drivel. You're striving for much better quality, while learning things for the first time, so make sure you're not rushed in the process.

Gathering the Troops:
Behind the Camera or in Front?

Although you could probably just turn on your webcam and clip your nails and someone would watch it on YouTube, you'll need other people to help out if you want to make a bona fide program.

It's not essential that every person in your group knows what they're doing — everyone has to start somewhere — but it is important that all of you are able to work easily together. So, if you are the director, it's best not to pick the person you have a huge crush on to run the camera, as you can't afford to have your mind turning to mush in the middle of a shoot. Gather people you like and who are capable of showing up on time and working for more than five minutes together without dissolving into giggles.

Once your crew is set, figure out what everyone is doing. First, choose the **director**. You'll probably automatically think, "Well, me of course! I'm the director and the star!" As tempting as that might be, consider picking one job or the other. Directing is a particular skill — it's seeing things from the outside, from the perspective of the audience. So, it's better if the director does not also play the lead role — that way, she can focus on observing. The director will tell you when things don't make sense or just aren't funny. A good director is organized, able to tell people what to do without sounding like an evil tyrant, and has a unique ability to understand when a show is good and when it starts to get stinkier than your brother's gym clothes. (See page 44 in the Play section for good tips on directing.)

If you're doing a scripted series, you'll need a **designated writer**. Many shows are scripted by a group with everyone coming up with the story together, but you'll need one person to put the ideas together into a coherent screenplay. It's important that the writer is good with words *and* really excited about the show — after all, it will be up to her to devise the script you need for shooting.

You'll also need a **cameraperson**. This job is perfect for your friend who's a photographer or comic book artist or has any other visual skill; although it may seem like a simple gig (all you have to do is point the camera at the action, right?), you'll often find that what turns a mediocre show or movie into a really great one is nicely framed shots. And don't forget that many people have hidden talents and just need a chance to flourish. So your friend who's mostly known for her skills on the basketball court may, in fact, turn out to be a great cameraperson.

Finally, your **cast**! This is the easy part. Who doesn't want to be on TV? The key here is to pick people for roles they will enjoy. If someone is complaining about being the gorilla-on-the-loose again, she probably won't give a great performance. Be willing to change people's roles, or even the premise of the show, if it gets your crew to be more enthusiastic.

Leader of the Pack:
Putting It All Together

One key to being a good producer or director is knowing how to use your crew's skills to full advantage—**work with what you have instead of trying to make something that is well beyond your means.** Take a hard look at your friends who want to make this show with you. In your head, you may have always dreamed of doing a cooking show à la Rachael Ray. But while planning the show, you realize that one friend does amazing skateboard tricks, another is a kung fu master, and another is a great painter. How can you use these skills together? Ditch the cooking show idea for now and instead dream up an action show in which the final battle pits a martial artist and a skateboarder, with a stylized backdrop expertly created by the painter. Or, try a talk show in which your friends demonstrate their skills and you interview them. Or, if you're set on a cooking show, you could at least use the skateboarder's skills by having her shoot what is called a "tracking shot," videotaping the action while rolling slowly along to create a feel of motion (while your cook furiously fries French toast). Something as simple as that tracking shot could elevate your show to the next level, and it was only through using your friends' skills that you were able to make that possible.

Who's On Board?

Every TV show needs:

director
the person who makes everything happen

screenwriter
she writes the dialogue and stage directions

cameraperson
she makes sure everyone looks good through good framing and lighting

editor
this person puts everything together at the end using a special computer program

cast
your team of actors

producer
she organizes the project and makes sure the crew shows up

"I think the people you work with have a huge impact on how your film turns out. I'd rather work with people that you not only get along with and trust but who actually want to get work done—than with people who slack off and are there for the wrong reasons."

—**Emilie Collier**, 19, filmmaker

Getting Started:
Making TV Really *Is* That Simple

This may sound weird, but the actual making of the show is the easy part. Once you've got a script, a cast, and an enthusiastic crew who're all on the same page, the technical problems are easily overcome. To make a TV show (or even an independent film) the only things you really need are a camera, a computer for postproduction editing, and someone to stand in front of camera. Despite all the bells and whistles and buff-looking people carrying around huge pieces of equipment that you see on big TV shoots, this is all you really need. And your camera doesn't have to be anything fancy. Your family's palmcorder can produce great results, though a bigger, fancier camcorder will allow you to do more tricks and make things look prettier. You can even get away with using the limited video abilities of a cheapo digital still camera, or even a cell phone, as long as your scenes are short. All of these devices use the same basic technology, so the process is more or less the same.

Here's what you have to do:
- preproduction
- shoot video
- capture video onto your computer
- edit scenes together
- output in a way people can watch

It'll be up to you to learn the quirks of your particular setup, but the below pointers should help any novice.

Preproduction

Unlike theater, TV and film are often shot without rehearsal. You're welcome to rehearse, and the show will certainly be better if you do, but because shooting video often involves lots of stops and starts and camera setups, rehearsals are not always effective. At the very least, you should read through the script together, though this obviously doesn't apply if you're doing an unscripted show. Scan the Play chapter for thoughts on generating content, auditioning, and rehearsing that can also apply to film.

To help the shoot go smoothly, directors will often prepare shot lists or storyboards before coming to the set. A shot list basically is a list of the kinds of shots that will be done that day. They might look like this in the script:

1. Interior of Theresa's room. Close-up of Theresa while her mom yells at her.

A storyboard looks like a comic strip and is made up of a series of drawings in boxes that represent all the shots for the script. Storyboards are helpful when making TV shows and totally essential when shooting something longer (like a full-length movie) in order to keep your shots, and your brain, in order.

1 2 3

Shoot Video

The two most important things about shooting video are light and sound. It doesn't matter how amazing every performance is, or if your friend does the most spectacular free-running leap off of a moving bus. If the people in the audience can't see or hear anything, they won't care. The lighting part is obvious, and most people won't shoot something if they can't see it. Sound, on the other hand, tends to be the sad and lonely member of filmmaking that always makes you pay for ignoring it later. In some ways, sound is more important than light. Think about it—if you saw a show with dark spots on the screen, or it was hard to see people's faces, you'd be annoyed but probably not mad enough to turn the show off if you liked it. Now imagine that there's an excruciating screeching sound running throughout the scene. Or that everyone mumbles so that you can't understand a word they're saying. A lot harder to watch, isn't it? A trick here is to keep a pair of headphones on at all times, so you can listen briefly to what you've just shot to make sure the audio is OK. If it isn't, shoot the scene over again! Your whole viewership could depend on it.

Capture onto Your Computer

Pretty much every basic computer comes with a free video editing program of some sort. If you have a Mac, it'll be iMovie, if you have a PC, then it's

Microsoft's Movie Maker. It doesn't really matter which kind you have, you still have to plug your camera into your computer with either a USB or FireWire cable (most regular video cameras will use FireWire) and capture what you've shot (transfer your footage onto the computer) through the program. If you are using a cell phone, then you'll probably have to track down how your particular phone plan handles getting video to your computer. One easy — but potentially expensive — solution is to mail the clips to yourself through the phone's web browser. If you have a Bluetooth cell phone, just transfer the files wirelessly to your computer.

Edit Scenes Together

Editing is where a lot of the art of television and filmmaking lies. All computer editing programs use something called a timeline on which you will put the footage you've captured and cut it down into clips. But these technical tasks are only one part of editing. A good editor must know how to most effectively arrange the clips, meaning how to make scenes move logically from one moment to the next. This takes some attention and thought. For instance, if one scene shows one person walking into a room and the very next shot shows her lying face down on her bed sleeping in different clothes, your audience will either think something magical has happened or that you are asleep yourself.

Audiences will carefully watch how shots are put together for clues as to what's going on, so you have to be specific about the clues you drop. Because almost no movies or shows — even talk shows and reality shows — unfold in real time, your viewers will use these clues to better understand time and space. For instance, if a character buys a plane ticket at a tourist agency, and then in the very next shot he is in a jungle, we'll assume he flew somewhere even though we never saw him on the airplane. Try to use shortcuts like this and a variety of camera angles to keep scenes interesting. A single take, or shot, of two people talking for five minutes about their trip to Hawaii will be boring onscreen. But cut back and forth to their faces and intercut some shots of Hawaii and the shark they're describing, and you have a more interesting scene.

Output

The last step, of course, is to output your show. There are several ways to do this. Are you making a MySpace or YouTube series? Or a video podcast for iTunes? If so, most programs have a way to export for uploading to the web. Maybe you want to make DVDs and distribute them to all your classmates? Again, all computers have a free DVD-making tool that's easy to use—on Macs it's iDVD, and on PCs it's DVD Maker. (You'll also need a DVD burner, which can be bought separately if your computer is not equipped with one.) Another possibility is to record to the tape in your camcorder using the same cable setup you used to capture the footage, then plug the camcorder into that 50-inch plasma screen your friend just got and watch it that way.

INSIDER TIPS
Shoot to Kill

Here are some basic rules for shooting.

Stay Centered on the Center

Viewers will naturally look at what's in the middle of the screen, so don't put a blue door in the center if you want us to watch who's talking on the left.

Get Coverage

Shoot a scene several times from several different angles and perspectives. Even if people are getting impatient, close-ups and shots of two people talking and long shots of the whole room will be a great help in the editing process. If you have two cameras and two camerapeople, you can get twice as much coverage in one take.

Double-Check

Check both the audio and video on your recordings frequently to make sure you have what you want before moving on to another scene.

Have Fun

Try shooting someone very tall from the floor to exaggerate their height, or zoom all the way out and then get very close to someone for a nice distorted, almost fish-eye effect. Be creative and experiment with different shots—it's the only way to learn.

INSIDER TIPS
Camera Tricks

Try these professional tricks for a more sophisticated show.

Green Screen

If you can get a slightly more advanced editing program like Final Cut Express or Avid Express Pro, shoot a scene against a green cloth or wall. In your editing software, there is a tool called Chroma Key, which will allow you to replace the green with whatever video you want. Make it look like you're swimming by filling the green space with undersea footage, or insert yourself into a Justin Timberlake video and make it look like you're performing together.

Tracking Shot

Have the cameraperson shoot from a moving shopping cart or other wheeled vehicle (like the aforementioned skateboard) for a great tracking shot. This is a very common and expensive technique in big movies and will make your show look professional. You can also get a licensed friend or parent to drive a car slowly while you shoot out the window.

Lighting F/X

Try different lighting techniques. Pointing lights up from the ground will make people look spooky, while a bright light coming through a window blind will make a great crime movie effect.

"The most important thing I've learned as a producer is that a creative approach to problem solving and negotiating is key—and that there are always many ways to do something."

—**Helen Hood Scheer**, professional TV producer and documentary filmmaker

Tricks of the Trade:
The Hook

O nce you have your TV show together, you need to figure out how to get people to watch it … in other words, find a hook! A hook is a quick snippet about your show that says why it is irresistible. Imagine you are in an alley between studio soundstages in Hollywood and run into an important cigar-chomping producer who wants to know what your great new show is all about. You've got one chance—one single sentence to sum up all of your show's coolness. What's it gonna be? Now imagine yourself as the cigar-chomper (well, maybe without the cigar)—would you go for a show that sounds like "Um, yeah, it's like a show where I'm with my friends and we, like, talk about stuff. And it's in my room and there are dances and stuff"?

You can put all the energy and creativity you want into a show, but without a good hook, people won't tune in. Need some help? See if you can recognize any of these hooks (answers are at the bottom of the page):

1· *A gripping terrorist thriller that unfolds over the course of one day, and each episode is one hour in that day.*

2· *A talk show where a tough-minded and yet gentle psychiatrist analyzes people and makes them cry on live TV.*

3· *A wildly diverse group of people miraculously survive an airplane crash on an island in the middle of nowhere and find that the island is a living, breathing thing.*

Notice how interesting all these shows sound without having to explain every detail about every person on the show. This is what you're looking for, something that will catch people's attention. Include your hook in YouTube descriptions, e-newsletters, flyers, and other places you are promoting your show. And if you do start dabbling in film, send your hook out to Hollywood producers whom you want to watch your new feature.

Answers: 1) 24, 2) Dr. Phil Show, 3) Lost

> *"For me, the hardest thing about working in documentary television is that there is always more work that can be done. I have a hard time putting my work to rest; I get too consumed by it."*
>
> —**Helen Hood Scheer**, professional TV producer and documentary filmmaker

Lights, Camera, Action!
Get Them to See It

Now that people are dying to see your show, give them a way to tune in. The simplest way to screen your show is on one of the many video upload sites like iFilm, YouTube, or MySpace. Still, although these sites make it easy for lots of people to watch your show, they often come with blurry video and tinny audio. **You don't have to be confined to the Internet if you don't want to be.** You can also make a DVD of each episode and

pass them around at school and in your neighborhood. If you have friends whose families own stores, ask them to put out a little box with free copies of your DVD, or make your show a weekly event at a friend's house if you know someone who has a good television or digital projector. Invite tons of people over and play the new episode. Then you have a social event as well as a TV show.

If you live in a bigger town or city, there's probably a cable access station whose sole mission is to provide an outlet for people in the community to broadcast their own shows. Call them up and ask for the submission requirements, and before you know it you might even have a show on real cable.

Selling Out Without Selling Out:
How to Raise Funds

Until you start getting people interested in your series, it's probably unlikely you'll have much luck raising money. With so many TV stations and YouTube and everything else, your friends may be hard-pressed to come up with a reason they should pay for something they can get elsewhere for free. On the other hand, **if you can get people hooked, start having screenings at your house** with free cookies or something and charge people for entry. (Or make the screening free and charge for the cookies!) You could even try to get them to subscribe to a series, then pass out DVDs to subscribers every month or week or however often you want. There are also video sites like Google that offer ways to sell your video online, but you'll need to get your parents involved in any financial transactions you do over the Internet.

"The hardest thing for me about doing film and video is being a girl in a male-dominated industry. It's a lot of fun to go to work on a project and not have to worry about drama and gossip because you are working with mostly guys. But that's the thing. It's hard to state your opinions and stand up for what you want to make when all of these guys think you can't do anything. It's been hard to overcome the whole stereotypical 'girls can't do anything,' but by being strong and having passion for what I want to make and what opinions I want to voice, I have held my ground in a male-dominated industry."

—**Emilie Collier**, 19, filmmaker

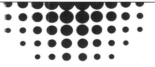

5 create an ART EXHIBIT

"The most rewarding thing about having a gallery is the knowledge that I am making a difference in both artists' and collectors' lives. It is a very difficult thing to be an artist in America and in this century, and I am satisfied to help in that struggle."

—**Lisa Chadwick**, owner of Dolby Chadwick Gallery, San Francisco

Finding the Next Van Gogh

You know that friend who sketches in her notebook during class or always doodles in the margins of her homework? She draws really cool mutant amphibians and overgrown daisies—but her sketches seem to be confined to the pages of her biology section? What about your buddy who draws beautiful trees or perfect portraits of people on the bus? The artists in your life may still be in high school, but that doesn't mean they shouldn't be recognized.

So how does a young artist get her work out there? While most people think of books and museums as places to exhibit artists' work, both of these venues usually pay tribute to people who are *already* famous. **Art galleries are the places where artists get discovered.**

Operating as both an exhibit and a place for artists to sell their work, galleries are an interesting cross between stores and museums. A good gallery show will draw art enthusiasts, snag the attention of the press, *and* attract buyers, so it is a great thing for a young artist to be a part of.

There's little difference between professional artists who exhibit in galleries and your talented friends, apart from the fact that your friends haven't yet had the opportunity to publicly express their visions. Why not help them out by opening your own art gallery, with rotating exhibitions of your friends' and even family members' work? And if you're a budding painter, sculptor, or graphic designer, feel proud to include your own work in the exhibit, too!

What You'll Need

- ✓ a venue
- ✓ art
- ✓ tools (hammer, nails, poster tape)
- ✓ party decorations
- ✓ music

r

"The thing that makes me happy as an artist is the look on people's faces when they can relate to my artwork—like they make a personal connection with it. That's what makes me the happiest."

—Jacqueline Calhoun, 17, multimedia artist

RESOURCES

www.teenink.com/art
A great gallery of art by teens online.

redstudio.moma.org
The teen section of the Museum of Modern Art's website, which includes interviews, interactive activities, and conversations about art.

www.arttable.org
A national organization for professional women in the visual arts.

www.aswexpress.com
An online store with a huge selection of discount fine art supplies.

First Things First:
Where's It Gonna Be?

Finding a space for the experience of visual-art viewing should not be taken lightly. Imagine if the first time you saw the Mona Lisa you were standing in a dark basement and bugs were crawling up your legs. You wouldn't be focusing on the mystery of her smile, now would you? These days, when people think they get all the visual stimulation they need from TV and the Internet, it's especially important to make live-art viewing a unique experience.

When choosing a venue, it's best to start with a place that has a daily, built-in audience because, unless it is summer or you have decided to fail the semester, you won't be there to supervise the exhibit at all times. Lots of **cafés** love having art on their walls, and they'll be eager and happy to go along with your gallery idea—especially if you promise an opening (and even closing) party where lots of people will come dressed up and ready to order cappuccinos. When it hosts an exhibit, the café gets to beautify its business *and* bring in more customers with one stroke. And cafés already have the right atmosphere for contemplating art because they are generally full of culture vultures who like to spend long periods of time sipping coffee and staring at the walls (which are usually decorated with someone's art, so why not yours?).

Another option is school. A **classroom** that is unoccupied most of the time is a great place for a gallery because students can pop in between classes. You can also hang art in the **hallways**, in the **cafeteria**, and even in **locker rooms**, as long as you get permission first.

Your **garage** or **basement** or **unused shed** might make a nice art space; even consider transforming your **bedroom** into a temporary gallery. You'll be surprised at how many available spaces there are, once you start looking. As you walk through your daily life, imagine art on the walls of everyplace you go. Eventually, the dream spot for your first art show is bound to appear.

Gathering the Troops:
Calling for Submissions

A curator is someone who puts together an exhibit in either a museum or a gallery. Curators sift through all the art that's out there, choose a select number of pieces, and present them in an enjoyable way. Using their knowledge of art and some instinct, they develop shows that say something about both art and the world around us. Here are a few ways to gather artwork for your show.

1. By theme. One way to curate a show is to collect art submissions around a certain theme. Maybe everyone's been concerned about what's happening in a foreign country. Ask your artist friends to create something or submit a piece they've already done on that theme. Or, you may notice that there is already a theme present in some of your friends' work, like maybe an obsession with the same celebrity, sport, or music. Start with their art and solicit more stuff with that theme.

2. By invitation. If you have a long list of artists that you like, invite them to partake in the exhibit instead of seeking general submissions. This cancels out the problem of having to reject people, but it also keeps the pool narrow, so you may want to open it up further next time.

3. By age. You can also curate exhibits by age (ask only freshmen to exhibit one month, then only 11th-graders the following month) or do an exhibit that's split between adults (parents, teachers, local artists) and teens on the same subject.

4. By generally good or interesting work. Simply collect submissions and include those you deem most promising or relevant to modern times in a show for up-and-coming artists.

> *"Do not second-guess yourself. Follow your own personal vision, and do not select art based on whether you think it will sell. Select art that you personally love and that is interesting for you."*
>
> —**Lisa Chadwick**, owner of Dolby Chadwick Gallery, San Francisco

INSIDER TIPS
How to Collect Submissions

As a curator, you will have to find a system by which to collect submissions from artists. Here are the two basic options.

Traditional Portfolios

This is typically a packet that consists of a sheet of slides of the artist's work, prints (copies) of the artist's work, or even original works on paper. They would be mailed to you, collected by you at school, or dropped off personally at your house. (Make sure you return them in good shape and in a timely manner.)

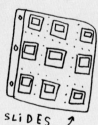

SLIDES ↗

↰ PORTFOLIO

Digital Portfolios

These are digital photos of the artist's work that can be emailed, burned onto a CD, or uploaded to a website. Digital portfolios are better than traditional ones because you are less likely to lose or accidentally damage an artists' slides or original work. Just make sure the images are high enough resolution that you can see them clearly.

You might also ask artists to submit an artist's statement, a common practice in professional galleries, in which the artist explains her intentions and techniques. You probably shouldn't make this an absolute requirement, though, because it may slow down the process; it can be hard enough just to get artsy types to remember to send their art!

Leader of the Pack:
Selecting the Artists

Being a curator can be a very satisfying occupation, and even artistic in its own way, since you get to decide what art goes into the exhibit and how it will all look together.

Taste in art is always subjective and you could fill a thousand pages or more debating what is art, what is craft, and what is just plain crap. People used to spit on the work of Vincent van Gogh. In his lifetime he never sold a single painting; now one will go for $80 million or more. Every generation makes something that the previous generation thinks isn't real art — it's taken forever for the mainstream media to accept that hip-hop is "real" music — so have an open mind when selecting work and view it not in comparison to art of the past but in its own right.

In fact, the great thing about having a gallery is that you get to answer the art question however you want. Maybe you know someone who makes cool shapes out of spoons in their spare time and another person who collects old signs and staples them together. Lots of people make great collages. Don't get caught up in wondering what's "real" art. Basically, the main thing that makes a piece of art gallery-worthy is that you think it is.

And don't let the often male-centered art world dictate what you choose. In addition to traditional forms, like sculpture and painting, things like fashion design and embroidery make great additions to an exhibit. One example of a highly successful, unconventional female artist is Judy Chicago. To make her famed 1970s work *The Dinner Party* she used a lot of crafts many might not think of as "art," like sewing, china painting, and weaving. The installation, which celebrates great female historical figures, has been shown in museums all over the world.

Artists can be sensitive, so when you do have to reject one because of lack of wall space or because her work doesn't fit your theme, lessen hurt feelings by assuring them that there will be future opportunities and by telling them that you will keep them in the loop for the next exhibit.

Who's On Board?

Every gallery needs:

curator
the person who chooses the art

exhibit designer
she figures out where to place or hang the art

party planner
the one who organizes the opening party

talent
DJs, musicians, whoever else you have performing at the party

promoter
she gets the word out about your exhibit

Getting Started:
Setting Up Your Space

While the curator selects the art, the exhibit designer organizes and hangs it. Sometimes the same person will do both jobs. Exhibit designers put a lot of thought into what pieces should go where and how a space looks and feels. It's kind of like being a DJ, but you're selecting and spinning paintings and crafts instead of songs. If you've chosen a café or some other venue that's already decorated, you may be limited in what you can do, but still keep these important elements in mind.

Light!

This is the absolute top priority. Use lots of pleasing light and preferably incandescent (regular lightbulbs) over flourescent (those long tubes) because fluorescent light doesn't reveal all the colors in the spectrum. A completely blue and red painting might come out looking a sickly green in flourescent light. Some galleries like to have lots of natural light streaming in through windows, while others have a general dimness with strong lights on the art alone, creating a hushed effect. It all depends on your taste—just make sure the art is visible! (See the following page for specific lighting tips.)

Placement

Where you hang a painting or place a sculpture can have an impact on a viewer in the same way a camera angle in a movie can change how you feel about the action. Putting a small painting way up high will make people crane their necks and peer into the distance, perhaps emphasizing the alienation the artist felt. Crowding a lot of art together might show there was communal effort involved. However you exhibit the art, be sure to consult with the artist. Some will want to be involved in everything, including the size of the nail that holds up the painting. These things may seem petty to you, but artists take their work very seriously and usually know how it will look best. To get the best results, hanging art should be a collaboration between the curator, exhibit designer, and artist.

Ambience

Do you want people to lounge around and contemplate the art alone, or stand in groups and discuss the work? Think about this as you place chairs or plan the route people take as they go from piece to piece.

> *"When you're in a gallery show, always stand by your artwork so you can talk to the viewers who may have a question or two about your art."*
>
> —**Jacqueline Calhoun**, 17, multimedia artist

♠ Tricks of the Trade:
Selecting the Right Lights

Because lighting is so important to how an art show looks, it's worth examining different kinds of illumination.

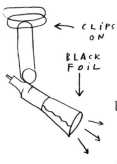

Clip-On Lights

You can get these at most hardware stores for fairly cheap and clip them onto any solid post or pipe. They aren't very focused lights but can be aimed somewhat. Focus light more by taking tin foil (or black foil, which can be bought at a photography store) and crimping it around the outside to form a hood on the light that is pointed at the artwork. Use electrical tape to secure the foil.

Flashlights

Take a normal flashlight and use duct tape to attach it to the back of a chair or a place on the ceiling, and point it toward the artwork. You can use foil here, too, to further focus the light.

Windows

If you've chosen a space with lots of windows, direct this light by hanging white sheets strategically on the wall that receives the most light. The light will bounce off the sheets toward whatever is on the opposite wall.

From Above

If all you've got is normal overhead lights and lamps, there are still ways to work with them. For instance, you can focus the light of a regular desk lamp by putting foil around the edges, and you can do the same with lots of ceiling fixtures or track lighting. Also useful are those reading lamps that have movable arms and lights that can be pointed at different angles.

INSIDER TIPS
Art in So Many Words

It's essential to tag every piece of work in the gallery so that viewers can get acquainted with the art. Here are some things the tags should include.

1 · Title of Artwork
If there isn't a title, just write "Untitled" and be sure to include the rest of the pertinent information.

2 · Name of the Artist
This is pretty self-explanatory; the artist can choose to use a pseudonym if they like.

3 · Materials
These are the materials and surfaces that were used to make the work. For instance, "charcoal and magazine cuttings on cardboard."

4 · Year
If the artist ever makes it big, whoever buys the art will want to be able to say "I had a piece she made way back in 2008!"

5 · Price
This is actually optional, though you should consider putting some kind of price on every piece, even if it's just 50 cents, unless the artist does not want to part with it.

 While it's important to get this basic information across, you and the artists can also have fun with making tags, including their own words about what they were thinking when they made the piece, a small artist statement, or even a small poem or humorous piece of text that the artist would like to have presented with the work.

Lights, Camera, Action!
Who Cares About the Art, Look at My Dress!

The best part of making a gallery is throwing opening parties. **Who knows why, but art just inspires great gatherings.** People are surrounded by interesting conversation pieces, so those awkward pauses you have at a regular house or school party are totally eliminated. Everyone is engaged and having a good time, and the art provides much better decor than the old neon Coca-Cola sign in your basement. The artists will be nervous and excited, adding an extra layer of energy. Play some good music and provide nice beverages and snacks so that people linger and really absorb the art in between dancing and chattering away.

If your exhibition is thematic, make the party thematic too. For instance, if it's all animal art, ask people to dress up as zebras and lions, or decorate with tropical plants. **People who come to an art opening are expecting things to be interesting and different, so don't be afraid to try something crazy.** This is the part where you get to be the artist (in addition to possibly exhibiting art yourself), so let your imagination soar.

And remember to be attentive to your artists. People who are selected and showing their art for the first time can be very nervous, so the more you can do to create a fun event for their grand opening, the better. Be encouraging and make sure you bolster every artist's confidence with a deluge of compliments.

"I believe gender no longer plays any role in being a successful art dealer, thanks to the multitude of women who have forged this ground ahead of me."

—**Lisa Chadwick**, owner of Dolby Chadwick Gallery, San Francisco

¢ Selling Out Without Selling Out:
How to Raise Funds

Most art galleries put prices on their art, as galleries are stores as much as they are exhibit halls. Although you won't be able to charge the steep prices they do, it can be fun to buy and sell a piece of art, if the artist is down with that. Ultimately, you and the artist would work together to come up with the price of the piece, and you can work out a sharing of the money, which in a case like this would probably be about 80 percent (artist) – 20 percent (you). But remember **the real goal is to get the art out there**, so do keep the prices as low as you can manage without insulting the hard work of the artist (not to mention expensive materials!).

Think about raising money for your gallery by selling food at the opening night party or little pieces of practical art (like birthday cards or coasters) made by the contributing artists.

"Don't get discouraged if you can't find a buyer to sell your artwork to, or if someone doesn't like your art, because the only critique that matters is your own."

—**Jacqueline Calhoun**, 17, multimedia artist

6 form a DANCE TROUPE

"**I love working with the body,** especially during a point in history when our bodies are often so neglected. Dance is a gentle reminder that we still reside in the house of the body."

—**Jodi Lomask**, artistic director of Capacitor Dance Group, San Francisco

Get Into the Groove

Is there any girl on the planet who hasn't at one time or another made up a dance routine with her best friends to their favorite song of the moment? Well, maybe. But chances are, if you're reading this you're not her.

You know, it doesn't take even one dance class to be able to choreograph complicated maneuvers and perform them totally in sync with your friends. By mixing hip-hop, pop, cheerleading, and whatever else, you've probably created some great moves that deserve to be seen by others. **And, in fact, if you watch dance squads for professional sports or background dancers in music videos, none of them are doing things you haven't already done.**

The problem is no one ever sees your dances! Most of the great choreography you dream up remains behind closed doors, preserved only in your memories (and maybe some grainy cell phone video) and viewed by no one, except a spying younger sibling. So, why not put together a group of friends to perform your killer routines? This is how great dance trends take off anyway — the Twist, breakdancing, the Macarena, you name it, they all got started by young people dancing in basements, on street corners, and wherever else the rhythm took hold.

What You'll Need

✓ boom box/sound system
✓ rehearsal space
✓ costumes

BOOM
BOOM
BOOM

"The most important thing I've learned about dancing is that everything looks better when you act like you know what you're doing. Even if you can't get a move down, if you dance with energy and enthusiasm, you will look good, and totally together."

—Katya Shackleford, 17, dancer

RESOURCES

www.young-dancers.org
This is a great resource specifically for young people interested in dancing.

www.bustamove.com
This site has lessons in all kinds of dancing, including hip-hop, swing, and lots of other cool stuff you can weave into your own routine!

✳ First Things First:
Your Motion Is Your Emotion

When deciding what kind of dance you are going to create, keep these two things in mind: movement and music.

Movement

The great thing about dancing is that it can express, without words, exactly how you feel about yourself and the world around you. So it's important that you let the music move you to do things unexpected and uniquely you. Studying other dance or borrowing moves from a highly energetic cheerleading routine or a well-choreographed music video is a great way to refine your techniques and get new ideas—but it should always be a jumping-off point for making up your own stuff.

In the beginning, it's also good to have a conversation about dance with your group to talk about your likes, dislikes, visions, and influences. But don't get too attached to your early ideas. **You don't have to decide to do a revolutionary hybrid of hip-hop, jazz, and Japanese butoh before you even begin practicing.** It's better to choose some music and then see what happens when you and your girls hit the dance floor.

Music

Good music is essential to making good dance. But dancing to an obviously defined beat (like the pounding drums of hip-hop or rock) is actually a relatively new trend and not one you have to stick to. Don't be afraid to experiment with alternative types of music. There's no reason why a great dance can't be choreographed to an old Frank Sinatra tune or a punk song rather than the standard electronic beats everyone dances to in clubs. And you can always mix music and dance traditions. Nā Lei Hulu I Ka Wēkiu, a famous Hawaiian hula troupe, performs traditional dances set to songs like Lauryn Hill's "Killing Me Softly." And Savion Glover, a famous tap dancer, sets traditional routines to everything from modern jazz to hip-hop. Experiment with different influences and stir several flavors into the mix—you never know what amazing sounds and moves might come out of it.

Gathering the Troops:
Selecting Fellow Booty-Shakers

Sometimes the group is just you and your best friend, and that's OK—just look at Fred Astaire and Ginger Rogers. But if you're a leader in a community of girls who like to move, you may run into a problem: Lots of people will want to be in your dance group. While it's hard to choose who among your friends will be in the group, it's even harder to arrange practices and performances for dozens of girls, let alone get everyone in sync! It's probably best to start with a max of six people, just to make it easier for everyone to stay on the same page in terms of dance movements and style. So how to choose your dancers without losing all of your friends? Here are some recruitment suggestions.

Informal Recruiting

If you simply want to ask friends and acquaintances to dance with you (rather than hold auditions), it's best to look for people who have something to say with their bodies, as opposed to selecting girls based on who's most popular, athletic, or practically a professional dancer. If your friend amazed you with her dance moves at a party, or the lead in the school play marveled you with her grace, start with one (or both) of them. Another idea is to invite a few friends over to bust some moves in your basement one weekend and see who's into it. You never know who will turn out to have the slickest moves or the most enthusiasm, or simply come up with your best costumes.

Auditions

When you form any kind of group, there's always the danger of hurting someone by not including them. The nice thing about auditions is that they give everyone the same chance. If an unpopular girl unexpectedly gives an amazing performance, you'll almost have to bring her on the team.

To audition dancers, ask each girl to prepare a dance to a one-minute piece of music they like. Use a spacious room and have everyone else wait outside while each dancer performs. Politely thank each person, being sure not to raise or crush anyone's hopes before you've made your selections. And remember that auditions are a nerve-wracking and painful experience for most people. Treat people respectfully and encourage everyone regardless of skill level. Unless you have hundreds of people auditioning, it's also well worth your time to get back to people personally rather than posting a list of those who made it. Those little touches can make a huge difference.

Group Auditions

An alternative to holding standard auditions for one group is to have general auditions for several groups. This is a great option for inclusiveness since everyone gets placed somewhere. Just make sure there are other girls interested in heading up the other groups—one will be enough for you to handle on your own. You can eventually join all groups together for a big performance at the end of the year or stage a friendly dance competition (or "battle") in which lots of groups take the stage at once.

Who's On Board?

Every dance troupe needs:

choreographer(s)
the ones who come up with the dance steps —
doesn't have to be one person

dancers
they dance, what else?

costume designer
she creates the right look for your troupe

stage manager
the one who handles lights, music, rehearsal schedules,
contact lists, and that sort of thing

emcee
the person who introduces each dance,
or the dancers, by name

Leader of the Pack:
Learning to Choreograph

Choreographing a dance starts from a mixture of both what's outside and inside the dancer—you'll want to trust your instincts about how the music moves you, but also keep your eyes open to the world around you. Aside from using existing moves you like, **base new dance moves on the way someone gets ready for bed or on the flight of a giant bird**.

Start by demonstrating to the group a new step you made up, or by just performing some instinctive movements. When demonstrating something to the group, let your feelings be your guide, not your judgment about how dorky you might look. Think about how krumping, the crazy hip-hop dance, must have started. The movements alone seem almost like seizures, but combined with the music and the intensity of feelings felt from the performers the dance becomes an amazing performance to behold. Still, in the beginning, someone probably just went on to the dance floor and started spazzing out.

Don't be afraid to do that, too! The rest of the troupe will be inspired by your willingness to try new stuff if you demonstrate steps with enthusiasm and confidence. The other dancers may even surprise you and come up with their own cool movements. In many companies, choreography is a collaborative process that brings a group closer together (dancers speak to each other through movement), so involve as many members as possible in making up the dance.

"I would encourage a new choreographer to spend time exploring her particular take on things. What makes an artist interesting is not the content, but her perspective."

"It is harder for women to find a style of directing and leading that works for them. It is very tricky. You need to be strong but not oppressive."

—**Jodi Lomask**, artistic director of Capacitor Dance Group, San Francisco

Getting Started:
Putting the Moves Together

After you've been practicing moves for a while with your group, it's time to actually put together a routine. The choreographer can collaboratively do this with the group or come to them with an already planned dance. Here are some techniques choreographers use to create dances.

1· Start from a single move and build a dance from there.

2· Make a dance around something you saw outside—like an old lady being helped across the street or two dogs playing.

3· Try out the steps yourself before bringing them to the group. A great way to prepare for a rehearsal is to videotape yourself when working through the dance alone. This way, you can review what you're doing before taking the new steps to the group.

4· Ask fellow dancers to improvise their own movements during rehearsals and come up with ways to improve them and link them together.

To make a dance, you also need a language and an understanding of rhythm.

Language

Every type of dance has terms associated with it that help choreographers when they give instructions to dancers. For instance, a "demi-plie" in ballet always means a half bend of the knees, and "spirit fingers" in cheerleading always signifies that the cheerleaders are going to wiggle their fingers enthusiastically. If you are creating a whole new type of dance, you will need to invent a new set of terms or notations. For instance, you could name a move that involves rolling across the floor the "hot sweep." Then, when you want to include that move in a series, you just tell the dancers: "Here we do eight beats of the hot sweep."

Rhythm

Regardless of what language your group creates in order to communicate, you'll always speak in terms of rhythm. From hip-hop to ballet, the only way dancers can communicate and stay in sync is through rhythmic counting. So, when building your dance, be sure each part is counted out. For instance, you would say "4 beats of the swan dive, then 2 beats of the watermelon flip." Or whatever.

INSIDER TIPS
Finding Rehearsal Space

You can dance anywhere really, but when looking for a place to rehearse your routines, there are a few things you should keep in mind.

No Carpet

Many dance steps include slides and skids that are all but impossible on carpet. If your house doesn't have hardwood floors or a smooth-floored basement, try someone else's place or see if your school will let you use the gym or a classroom after school. (You'll probably need to get it approved by the principal.) If you must practice on carpeting, don't wear shoes. If you practice outdoors, choose concrete over grass.

Be Where You Can Be Loud

It's very hard to dance quietly, so look for spaces where a little noise won't bother anyone. If you live in an apartment, you're likely to drive the downstairs neighbors crazy with all of the jumping up and down and music-playing that goes along with dancing. Instead of having to tip-toe around, grab a boom box and head to the park or a community amphitheater.

Privacy

Trying out dance moves can be intimidating, and the last thing you want is for people to be self-conscious. Make sure your space is safe from passing foot traffic that might stare at or even tease you.

♠ Tricks of the Trade:
It's Really About the Hot Pants

Sure, your moves are what will move people—but don't forget to select good costumes. Since dance is a mostly nonverbal art form, everything that the audience sees will have a powerful impact, and **costumes can amplify the effect of dance moves—and even the story the dance is telling—if selected thoughtfully.** Probably the best person to design costumes would be one of the dancers; see who has ideas or is interested in fashion and ask if she'd like to be the costume designer.

Your costumes can be anything as long as they leave enough room for movement, but are not so loose that people can't see what your body is doing. You could come up with a unified theme—like your whole group could have matching colors but different outfits, or matching outfits in all different colors. Or everyone could be dressed as a different mythical creature, using only subtle accessories like ears and tails to get the point across. Or you may decide to keep everyone in the exact same costume. An easy and cheap way to do this is to print up a T-shirt for everyone (using iron-on transfers) that has the name or symbol of your troupe, then all wear the same color skirts, pants, or tights. However you dress up your troupe, keep in mind that the costumes are an essential part of the dance that people will pay lots of attention to.

Lights, Camera, Action!
Taking It to the Streets

When your gig is polished, or almost, you should start looking for a venue. The cool thing about dancing is that it can be done anywhere. A theatrical space with lights and a great sound system is the ultimate dream, of course, but don't let the difficulty of finding a real theater stop you. **Most of the great dance moves of all time were developed at performances in warehouses, art galleries, basements, or just out on a street corner.**

All you really need to put on an amazing show is a boom box and a flat open space. Your local park may have an amphitheater you can use—just be sure to check with your city's parks and recreation department (ask if you need a permit). Or use your back patio if you have one and it's big enough—just put out a few chairs for the audience or make it a standing-crowd thing. Lots of students are allowed to use the cafeteria after school, but you'll need to talk to school administrators about that. Try registering your dance troupe as an official after-school club for access to facilities. It doesn't matter where you dance, just dance!

> *"The hardest thing about dancing, for me, is confidence. It's difficult to stop worrying about what you look like and just try. But that's what it takes to learn and improve."*
>
> —**Katya Shackleford**, 17, dancer

Selling Out Without Selling Out:
How to Raise Funds

While most dancers do it for the sheer joy of it, there's no reason you can't also raise a little money for costumes or a better sound system. Charging for tickets is an obvious choice, though you may want to start out with a "suggested donation" until you make a name for your troupe. **Try joining up with your art show (page 70) pals for a combined show of performance and art and split the proceeds.** There are also dance competitions with cash awards. To find out how to enter, check your local youth information pages in newspapers and the many online youth dancing resources.

7 launch a FASHION COMPANY

> **Even in fashion, where the bulk of buyers are women,** the very top couture designers and top fashion houses are run by men. Most of the profits are made by men. There may be times that you are the only woman in the boardroom. Don't be afraid to wear a suit. Not a lavender pantsuit, but a man's suit with a great dark tie. This may seem like a game, but it has given me confidence before. It says 'I am not asking for special treatment' or 'I am your equal.'
>
> —**Tacee Webb**, project manager of American Apparel and founder of Fashion Design Camp

The Shirt Off My Back

At one time or another, almost every girl has felt some frustration with the modern fashion world. One-size-fits-all (or no one) tops, too-skinny pants, and some random trend in shoes that leaves your feet screaming with blisters. And then there's the fact that you're paying to be tortured like this. Unfortunately, as much as you'd like to swear off clothes completely, that's not really an option. If you've had it with the clothing companies out there, it's time to start your own.

Does that mean you need to become an expert seamstress? Nah. You don't even need to know the difference between an A-line and a boot cut. **The best kind of fashion business to start is a re-fashion business, where you take clothes people already have and redesign them.**

Re-fashioning is not a new concept. It started with the hippie scene of the '60s and has reappeared with every generation, from the punks of the '80s to the glam queens of today.

Anything is possible. Re-invent dated T-shirts by applying funky iron-ons. Dye a pair of tights purple and pair them with a new cutoff miniskirt.

By starting a re-fashion business, you get to use your creativity to express yourself, create wearable art, help the planet by recycling old clothes, and even make a few extra bucks. And getting customers shouldn't be too hard—who doesn't have a few items in their closet that could use a refresh?

What You'll Need

✓ lots of stuff!
See page 100 for a list of starter tools

"I love fashion because it makes me happy when I finally finish a garment and I see the final product being worn by a customer, and the customer says, 'It's exactly how I pictured it.'"

—Cassandra Rae Martell, 19, founder of Casey Rae Designer and Custom Clothing (*www.CaseyRaeDesigner.com*)

RESOURCES

www.craftster.org and www.getcrafty.com
Two great places to get alternative craft project ideas and show off your own creations.

Fashion 101: A Crash Course in Clothing
by Erika Stalder

Jeaneology: Crafty Ways to Reinvent Your Old Blues
by Nancy Flynn

Generation T: 108 Ways to Transform a T-Shirt
by Megan Nicolay

How to Desconstruct and Reconstruct the Clothes of Your Dreams
by Elissa Meyrich

First Things First: Gather Your Fashion Tools

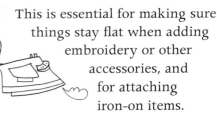

Though it's great to have advanced tools like a glue gun and a sewing machine, you really only need some basic things to get started reconstructing clothing. Here are tools and materials that are used in the techniques discussed later on in Tricks of the Trade.

Practical Tools:

buttons, snaps, clasps, and Velcro

You'll need these to keep things closed!

duct tape

This is that big, silver, super-strong kind of tape that plumbers and construction workers use. Yes, it's a fashion tool. People have been known to make entire jackets out of duct tape.

fabrics

You can pick up fabric odds and ends from most fabric stores, and it's cheaper than getting full yards. Ask what's available. If there's a leather shop in your town, they may give or sell you cheap little fragments of leftover leather.

fusible webbing

This is a net of fabric glue you use to stick cloth to other cloth. Some are made especially for certain fabrics, so be sure to get the type that fits your project.

iron

This is essential for making sure things stay flat when adding embroidery or other accessories, and for attaching iron-on items.

needles and sewing thread

This comes in many colors, textures, and thicknesses. In the DIY era of the '90s, folks used fishing line, but thread from the fabric store will do just fine.

safety pins

If it's good enough for punk rock, it's good enough for you!

scissors

This will be a primary tool. Be sure you have really high-quality, sharp scissors.

Decorative Tools:

acetate

These clear plastic sheets for sketching stencils are found in art or office supply stores. They are used for printing stencils from the computer or hand-tracing designs.

brushes

Find paintbrushes and foam rollers that are especially made for fabric paint.

dye

Cold-water dyes are easiest to work with, but if you are trying to change the color of a really dark fabric to a lighter color, you may need to use a hot-water dye.

fabric paint

Fabric paints come in zillions of containers, many of which have little roller heads or sponge brushes attached so that you can apply paint directly to the cloth. For these projects, just get a tub of a color you like with no special applicator—no need to get fancy.

iron-ons

These are sheets of paper made especially to iron onto clothing. Just get ones that fit your printer—you can find them at office supply and art stores.

spray paint

There are spray paints made especially for fabric, but any type will do. Just be sure your work area is well-ventilated.

"I first started my business at age 18; I would always get 'She's a little blond ditz' vibes from older women when trying to sell my clothing. I had to win their attention by showing them what I am made of and hiding my young identity as much as possible. After, it always ended in the response, 'I didn't know you were that good.' "

—**Cassandra Rae Martell**, 19, founder of Casey Rae Designer and Custom Clothing (*www.CaseyRaeDesigner.com*)

Gathering the Troops:
Operation Re-Fashion

The great thing about a re-fashion business is that anyone can participate. And most people love to sit around and chat while their hands are busy—witness the huge craze of knitting circles. Encourage your friends who think they aren't fashionable to participate. Perhaps they will discover their own style through the process!

Because of the varied nature of the work, you don't need to be super-selective about your team. Just make sure everyone is enthusiastic and willing to try new things. You don't want to work with a group of people who constantly shoot everything down as being "lame" or "weird-looking." If you are having trouble finding people to join you, post a flyer around school and announce your venture in class. The best way to recruit participants is to advertise some of your own creations by wearing them. If you've got it, flaunt it.

Who's On Board?

Every fashion company needs:

designer
the person who comes up with or organizes the group's overall design ideas—can be several people

sewers
the people who help sew and put things together

fabric painters
the people who do the stenciling and other fabric design

salespeople (optional)
the people who help pull in customers

models
the girls who talk the talk and walk the catwalk

Leader of the Pack:
You Are What You Wear

Even though you will eventually be making clothes for others, experiment on your own threads first. What matters most to you in clothing? Flashy colors? Comfort? Snug fit? Your clothing has to be a real expression of who you are, free of judgment and self-consciousness. The worst thing you could do is try to imitate a fashion you don't really like because other people think it's cool. A style becomes "in" not because it's selling in every store, but because the person who invented it (or the model she hires) is wearing it with complete confidence and flair. If you wear your new styles with confidence, other people will get into them, too.

Of course, it's possible that at first people will mock your new clothing, merely because they're shocked someone has stepped outside of the Abercrombie & Fitch prison. Though it may be painful at first, stick to your guns. If you look in the mirror and like what you see, people are missing the point and will eventually come around. Innovators often run into static at first and you'll need a lot of confidence when you start your business.

Designers often produce things that others think look ridiculous, but then their designs become part of a fad. Have you ever watched a real fashion show? A model may come walking down the runway in a burlap sack with something that looks like a trash can lid on her head. No one laughs, because they're looking at the lines of the "dress" and material of the "hat" and trying to figure out how they can adapt this look for their new fashion line. Encourage the rest of your friends who are involved to take risks with whatever they design.

When designing for other people, you'll want to stay true to your vision but also make something that suits them in particular. Even when people want what you've made for yourself—"I need to have a hat like that!"—you'll be working with clothing they already have, and different sizes, colors, and fabrics will call for different solutions. Besides, the main thing you have to sell is the imagination and creativity of your fashion company and the one-of-a-kind value of each piece, so you don't want to make everything exactly the same.

Getting Started:
Creating a Company

There's a lot more to starting a re-fashion company than just making the clothes (more about that in Tricks of the Trade). The point of a company is to:

1. Come up with a unified vision.

2. Create things with that vision.

3. Inspire the people who work with you to believe in and adopt your vision.

4. Sell your product (optional).

Creating a company with a vision is not as difficult as it may sound. **Your vision just has to be a unified thought that everything in your business reflects.** 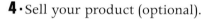 For example, your company could be called Re-fashion on the Fringe, and every item could contain some sort of fringe, or Fashion in the Know, and you would print words or sayings on all of your clothes. Or your vision could be more general: You could have humorous slogans on all your clothing, or everything could be unified by one particular color. What's most important is that you wholeheartedly believe in your vision.

Having your own company can be very rewarding because you're inspiring other people and expressing your creativity and vision to the world. But it does come with some obstacles. For instance, squabbles can (and often do) occur over artistic differences, how you choose to run your operations, what your products cost, and what your company spends money on. The best way to deal with these things is to be very open to change and to try to resolve conflicts peacefully while respecting everyone's point of view.

Not for Profit

If you decide to keep money out of the picture, there are lots of other things you can do with your finished fashion masterpieces: Offer your re-fashion services for free, sell stuff but donate all proceeds to your favorite charity, make clothes only for company members, enter fashion contests, or put on a fashion show. You don't need to make money to have a company.

For Profit

If you do start getting paid work, be careful that it doesn't cause tension among the company members. The best and simplest way to handle making money is to write up a contract that everyone signs, agreeing to what you decide to do with the profits, so there won't be any confusion or doubt in the future. The contract could say that everyone has to work a minimum amount of hours, that the profits go directly to buying more materials, or that all the money get split evenly. And keep everyone in the know about exactly what cash comes in and where it goes. In the business world, this is called transparency. Stay transparent, and your business will thrive. Check out the Small Business Administration, which has a special link for teens (*www.sba.gov/teens*), to get more info on necessary licensing, financial advisers, and other matters.

You must make sure everyone feels like they're getting treated equally. Lots of friends go into business together, and they succeed by respecting one another and keeping personal and financial matters as separate as possible.

To grow your business, get the word out. Make flyers, print and hand out business cards, and talk to local bands and dance companies that might be interested in your clothes.

♠ Tricks of the Trade:
Basic Techniques

Transforming old clothing is creative and fun. All of the techniques on the following pages are fairly simple and can be done on a variety of clothing. If you decide to get into more advanced projects that involve tools like sewing machines and hot glue guns, take the obvious safety precautions. The following are just ideas to get you started. Once you begin experimenting with these different techniques, invent some of your own combinations and designs.

Changing Colors

Dye is an easy way to change your clothing's entire look. Any cold-water dye will do. Just dunk the item in a plastic bucket or other container you're not worried about staining and follow the instructions on the dye. This works great with canvas shoes like All-Stars or any kind of cotton-based fabric. Remember that things will dye differently depending on the original color of the fabric. For instance, if your shirt is red and you add blue, it will turn purple. After you're done, throw the items in the dryer to set the dye. Don't put any other items in with the dyed clothing in case the color bleeds. If you cut off the edges of the canvas on your shoes before putting them in the dryer, you'll have a nice ratted effect.

Iron-On Images

When used correctly, iron-ons work great on most clothing, backpacks, canvas bags, and canvas shoes. Here are some ideas for iron-ons.

T-Shirts. Use a great artwork, like a Picasso or an Andy Warhol. (If you start making shirts based on someone else's work and selling them on the web or to stores, be sure to get the proper licensing.) You can also make your own images or use your own photos. Just download them and print them out on ink-jet iron-on paper.

Shoes. Celtic designs look particularly good on shoes, but anything with nice strong lines will work. Pick a design that wraps around the whole shoe. The trick here is to make sure the surface you're putting the design on is flat and can be ironed on to, so the ankle part of the high-top shoes are usually the best choice.

Celtic designs

Bags. You'll have to work with smaller images for backpacks—quirky icons or strange symbols make great additions to backpacks and can fit between pockets. You can do larger designs on the side of a canvas messenger bag or purse.

Stencils

With a couple of good stencils, you can make a design with a spattery effect that covers an entire shirt or pair of pants, escaping the size limitations of iron-ons. Make your own stencils by hand or with your computer and printer.

By Hand. Draw a bold-lined image on paper or cardboard, then tape a sheet of acetate to the drawing and cut along the lines. Remember that the spaces you cut out are where the paint will go, so don't only cut along the outside edges, but cut out any detail you want to show in the center (like the triangle in the letter "A," for instance).

By Computer. If you're more of a designer type, buy acetate that's the size of normal paper and print a digital image directly onto it from your computer printer. After printing, cut along the lines of the drawing on the acetate. For designs larger than a standard piece of paper, you'll need to print them out in sections on a few sheets and then tape them together. Not all printers are capable of outputting on acetate. If yours can't, still print out a design from the computer onto paper, tape the acetate to the drawing, and cut it out the same way you would if you had drawn it.

Once you have your acetate stencil, place it onto your shirt and fix it into place with pins or tape. Use a little foam roller to smooth fabric paint onto the stencil, or use fabric spray paint. Let the shirt dry completely before handling.

Personal Graffiti

Spray paint your clothes multiple colors, or use stenciled designs to create cool effects. Choose a stencil of a word and spray that on your T-shirt or jeans. Also cool is metallic spray paint — give yourself a pair of fabulous metallic shoes for $5! Sharpies (permanent ink pens) are good for more handmade art or self-tagging, especially on canvas shoes.

Painting Fabric

Aside from using fabric paints to color in your stencils, try free-painting just like an artist would on a canvas. Use a quality brush and a tub of fabric paint, and make a true artwork out of a shirt or bag or shoe.

Rip It Up!

This is easy. Simply cut the collar or sleeves off of a T-shirt, or for jeans make cuts on the legs or shave fabric off at the thighs with a knife or shaving razor. Or whatever looks good.

Decoupage

This is basically a way to stick something onto something else. In this case, you'll be sticking one fabric to another. You'll need your fusible webbing for this. Find a cool pattern you like on some old sheets or fabric, and cut out the images. Attach the fusible webbing to the back of the design, then iron onto your article of clothing. It's sort of like making your own patches. You can cover the obnoxious logo on your shoes (who wants to be a walking advertisement anyway?) with a cool retro '50s image, or add several designs to a skirt or pants to spice things up. Use only cotton fabrics for this, as the hot iron will melt other fabrics.

Lights, Camera, Action!
Have a Fashion Show

Now that your company has made some hot items, it's time to strut your stuff. One way to do that is to host a fashion show. The traditional version includes a raised runway with lots of gossipy folks snapping pictures and staring at hemlines, but yours doesn't have to fit that model. Use either a local theater or your school auditorium (with permission, of course). Or pick any available large room and have everyone who's not in the show sit on the floor (it's important for the models to be above everyone, so the whole outfit can be seen).

Just about anyone can be a model. **In fact, this is a great opportunity to promote the concept that a girl doesn't have to be a size zero to hit the runway.** Since only a tiny percent of the world looks like normal fashion models, most people will be relieved to see a diversity of shapes and sizes at your fashion show, especially since your different fashions will be designed for and look good on different types of bodies. And just because you plan the fashion show doesn't mean you can't be in it, too!

"Being positive is contagious. People want to buy good energy as much as they want to buy a beautiful dress or great jeans. People want to wear the experience and identity of what they have purchased. If your brand is a part of creating that feeling and memory, then they will want to wear clothing you made for them and sold to them all the time."

—**Tacee Webb,** project manager of American Apparel and
    founder of Fashion Design Camp

¢ Selling Out Without Selling Out:
How to Raise Funds

The obvious way to make money here is by selling clothes. So the question is, how much should you charge? At first, you may want to keep your prices low (just a little more than what the materials cost) so that you're able to build up a clientele. But once your business is rolling, charge more—some of these jobs can take a fair amount of time, and there's also the value associated with originality and creativity. While you don't want to price yourself out of the market, remember that many girls cough up hundreds of dollars for a pair of jeans at the mall. **You needn't feel embarrassed to charge a modest sum for something that's way cooler than what's for sale at the Gap.**

8 hold a POETRY SLAM

 I don't feel completely alive unless I'm creating—and poetry is the art form I seem best matched with because I love playing with words. Writing poetry gives me a way to reflect on life's awesome mysteries and its harsh realites.

—**Sarah Rosenthal**, poet and author

Poetry Is Hot

If you're a fan of words, you know how sweet it is when the right ones come together, whether in a love poem, a quirky limerick, or a rap. There's nothing quite like the sound of a dreamy verse, a catchy phrase, or a tight rhyme. But even though poetry pervades everything in our culture, from Hallmark cards to SUV commercials, we still tend to think of it as static, to be read in a book in an English class, usually after the writer has long been dead.

Yet poetry started as an art that was not only spoken, but also performed. Legend has it that thousands of years ago the famed Greek poet Homer wandered around speaking a poetic history of his people to whomever would listen. The rimur chanters of Iceland have passed along the poem-stories of their culture since people can remember. And the politically charged Beatnik poets of the '50s took to café stages in fiery readings and collaborated with jazz bands in an effort to bring their words to the masses and move poetry off the print-ed page and directly into your ears.

And then came slam poetry. With an often musical sound derived from hip-hop and alternative music, slam poetry exploded onto the scene in the late '90s and was popularized by the *Slam* and *Slam Nation* movies and Russell Simmons' TV series *Def Poetry*. Slam is a style of poetry that, like a monologue or a rap, is meant to be performed. A poetry slam itself is an event, and often a competition, that pushes writers to entertain as well as enrapture an audience with pounding poems about social culture, political causes, personal identity, and gender.

Slam poetry is intended to bring life to the written word and to share a vision, thought, emotion, or political idea in verse. If you love words and want to join others in a celebration of language, there's no better way than a poetry slam to gather community and get your girls to take center stage.

What You'll Need

- ✓ poets
- ✓ a venue
- ✓ paper and felt-tip pens (for scoring)
- ✓ microphone/amp (optional)
- ✓ decorations (optional)
- ✓ DJ/music (optional)

"What makes me most happy about doing slams is seeing people my age empowering themselves and each other with their words and being able to take part in that."

—Luara Venturi, 17, Youth Speaks poet

RESOURCES

www.youthspeaks.org
This nonprofit organization runs national teen poetry slam events; go to the site to learn more.

www.poetryslam.com
The official website of Poetry Slam Inc. Get all general information, as well as specific rules for slams, here.

First Things First:
Location, Location, Location

One of the essential parts of your planning is choosing the right venue. It's important to pick a place that's big enough to fit a nice-sized crowd, but small enough for the poets to be heard without a microphone and speakers (unless you have access to these).

When choosing a place, consider what kind of a vibe you want to establish at your slam. Public and power to the people? Do it outside on a street corner or in a park amphitheater and random strangers can watch. More organized and with good acoustics? School cafeterias and auditoriums work well if your principal approves, and many cafés and restaurants will be only too happy to host your event. You can even just set it up in your backyard or basement if there's enough room.

Whatever you do, stage your event in a place that will help increase the sense of excitement and energy in the audience. Lots of venues are good options. All you really need are poets and an audience, and everything else is gravy.

Gathering the Troops:
Recruiting the Poets

Poetry slams are as competitive as they are artistic, so when organizing your slam recruit fearless poets who are willing to be scored on their work. Your poets need to be as much performers as they are wordsmiths; even if someone has the best poem, she'll get slammed if she mumbles incoherently into the microphone without ever looking up. To start, you might want to ask people in the theater department, rappers you know, and other extroverted artistic types to join, and post flyers at school or advertise in your school newspaper. But not every participant need be the most outgoing person in the world. Like in karaoke, **many performers who start out shy start to kick butt once they find their groove**. So give anyone who has something to say a chance to participate—the more diverse the group of performers, the more interesting the slam.

When gathering your participants, you'll need to decide whether you want it to be an all-girls slam or co-ed. Since this is a competition, you'll have to face the fact that boys and girls often see competition differently. Boys tend to be more focused on winning at all costs, while girls are more willing to support each other, even in competition. And boys add other distractions, which you're probably well aware of. These stereotypes don't always hold true, but if you have some shy girlfriends who'd really like to read, there's a better chance they'll do so at an all-girl slam. Once you get comfortable, open it up to boys—or compete against them!

Who's On Board?

Every poetry slam needs:

organizer/producer
the girl who is in charge of finding the venue,
getting the poets together, and gathering a crowd

judges
they are audience members or invited community members

emcee
the one who introduces the poets, helps choose judges,
and gets the crowd amped

scorekeeper
the person responsible for keeping score

poets
the competitors

snack seller
the friend who sells refreshments (if allowed at your venue)
to help pay for the slam

> *"Don't let the scores invalidate what you have to say or discourage you from writing more poetry. Scores are only there to make things a little more exciting."*
>
> —**Luara Venturi**, 17, Youth Speaks poet

INSIDER TIPS
Judges and Scoring

A slam is typically a competition, which means you need to have judges and scoring methods.

Choosing Judges

In poetry slams, there are always five judges in total. The judges are mainly chosen at random from the audience—the emcee will ask for volunteers and choose a diverse group of people. In teen slams, like the ones produced by Youth Speaks, one or two guest "celebrity" judges—like a local librarian, writer, or politician—are often included. Guest judges help raise the profile of your event and inspire the poets to be more impressive. You could even bring your principal in if he or she is down with some creative chaos.

Scoring

Each judge writes down a score from 1–10 on a piece of paper and holds it up when the poet is done. The highest and lowest scores get dropped, and the poet receives the sum of the three middle scores. The emcee keeps track of all the scores throughout the night and announces the winner at the end.

There are no real rules governing the scoring of poetry, but judges should take into account tone, cadence, sophistication of rhymes, poem content, the reader's stage presence, and an audience's reaction to a poem. While audience members at a teen slam are seriously discouraged from booing an actual poem (it's about celebrating poetry, not putting it down!), audience members can vocally agree or disagree with the judges' scores. Though the judges can't change the score given for that poem, they may take the feedback into account when scoring the same poet the next time around.

Leader of the Pack:
How to Organize a Slam and Pick an Emcee

If the slam is your idea, you'll likely be organizing (producing) it. That requires getting poets together and filling certain other roles.

One of the most important roles to fill is the emcee. **The emcee is the person who introduces the poets, keeps things interesting when no one is performing, and oversees the judging.** As the organizer, you are the best choice for emcee because you know the event better than anyone else. But if you're not the charismatic type or don't want to be on stage for the entire event, choose someone who better fits that role.

An emcee must keep things moving without ever letting any silence fall over the room. The emcee:

- introduces the poets with their bios (which could be written humorously by the poets for some comic relief)

- rushes to the mic after each poet performs and encourages the audience to give another big round of applause

- fills stage time in between poets by saying funny stuff or even reading her own short poems

- brings the whole event together and helps poets feel more confident and have a better time

To keep things exciting, and to keep your emcee from totally passing out from exhaustion, employ two emcees who can play off one another, taking turns when they get tired.

You might also have a DJ at the event (or someone simply manning an iPod that's connected to speakers) to play music in the background whenever nothing's happening onstage. Music can also be used to introduce poets, like in baseball, when players have particular songs they want played in the stadium before they bat.

As the organizer you'll need to spend a lot of your time motivating the competitors. The emcee as well as the poets will need to hear as often as possible that their poems are awesome, that they look great, and anything else nice you can think of.

Getting Started:
How It Works

The basic rules of a poetry slam:

1· Poems can be no longer than three minutes.

2· Five judges are chosen randomly from the audience (or invited by the organizer).

3· All poems read must be original pieces.

4· No props or costumes are allowed.

5· Of the scores the poet receives from the five judges, the high and low scores are dropped and the middle three are added together, giving the poet a total score of $0-30$.

There are several different ways to do this, of course. Here are a few.

1·Organize it around a central idea
Sometimes the themes are empowering, like "Why I Don't Need Drugs," and sometimes they're goofier, like "Poems About Oatmeal." Providing a theme may inspire reluctant writers to participate.

2·Just make sure the theme is pretty loose and open-ended
A good theme is "What Music Means to Me." A not-so-good-theme is "Write a Poem About Death Cab for Cutie Because They're My Favorite Band." You want

to inspire the poets, not restrict them. Pair your slam with a charitable cause. For instance, you could choose the theme "No Dogs Allowed" and raise money for the local animal shelter.

3 · Compete in teams

It could be different classes at your school that are competing, or different schools in your town. No matter what, the judges chosen from the audience shouldn't be involved with either team.

4 · Go pro

If you want to get serious about it, apply to do a slam in conjunction with a larger organization like National Poetry Slam, or the teen-centered Youth Speaks. Then your winners can move on to regional competitions. Some of these larger organizations may have specific rules or formats you need to follow, so get all of the details beforehand.

Whatever kind of slam you do, you will need a scoring system. Here are two ideas.

1 · Hold it in rounds

If there are 10 readers or teams in the first round, the top four scorers move on to the next round and compete against each other with new poems. Then, the top two scorers compete in a finals round, and the winner gets the grand prize. (The runners-up get the less-than-grand prizes.)

2 · Have a one-off

Everyone reads one poem each, and a winner is chosen. This works when the writers have less time to prepare or there is less time for the slam overall. For instance, if you were doing an impromptu slam as part of an art gallery benefit, the slammers would have to quickly write something based on the art.

Because of the competitive nature of a slam, be sure to keep the tone light. The emcee is crucial in making this happen. Although the audience is encouraged to be vocal, the emcee needs to keep insults at bay. The competition should be good-natured, because in the end it's all celebrating poetry, right?!

FIRST

PLACE

♠ Tricks of the Trade:
Honing Your Craft

So, now that you're organized and have your slam together, you might want to focus on your writing.

The good news about slam poetry (also known as spoken word) is that it does not need to be written in iambic pentameter. It does not need a set amount of lines or syllables or verses. Even rhymes, which add a nice cadence that can wow your audience with verbal fireworks, aren't necessary to write a slam poem. So what makes a good slam poem? Here are the four main guidelines to follow when crafting your masterpieces.

1. Make them see it

Try, whenever possible, to use visual language. Describe things specifically, so the listeners can be swept away into your world. So, for instance, instead of saying, "She expressed a lot of emotion and it made me sad," try, "There was anger crackling from her eyes like fireballs, and my world caught fire and collapsed into a thousand flaming waterfalls."

2. The power of sound

When you are reading a poem aloud, you have to take sound into special consideration. There are certain words that just sound great when paired up and spoken aloud. **Instead of filling your poem with long words that you don't really like or know that well, choose words that roll off your tongue in a way that makes your poem sound like music.** Sometimes this means using rhyme, other times alliteration (same letter starts several words in the sentence), and other times repetition. Experiment with different poetic techniques and don't be afraid to invent your own.

3. Mean it

Your poems will be more meaningful to the audience if they actually mean something to you. Don't be afraid to get personal in your poetry, or really put your opinions out on the table as long as they don't personally disrespect other people. (It's OK to write about gender discrimination, but it's not OK to write a four-letter-word-filled rant about how much of a jerk that guy in your class is, adding a few unsavory comments about his mom, and finishing the poem off with his name and phone number.)

4 · Read up

If you want to really perfect your craft, the best thing any poet can do is read work by other poets (and great lyricists too). Get an idea of what is out there. Attend other slams. The point is not to copy other people, but to look for influences that will get your brain and heart moving. **All great artists take inspiration from great artists that came before them — knowing your craft is the first step to perfecting it.**

And Don't Forget

Read your poem with the same care you took to write it. Whatever rhythmic pattern or poetic techniques you use for your poem, emphasize them with your voice when reading. If there are several rhymes bunched together, try pumping up the intensity as each rhyme hits. For inspiration, listen to rappers and other slam poets and pay attention to how they use their own vocal rhythms to set themselves apart.

"The hardest thing about sharing my poetry at readings is how vulnerable it feels. Let's face it, I'm pretty much turning my brain inside out for the audience to see, so there's a fear that if they reject the poem, they reject me ... If I can just accept feeling vulnerable, and let the audience see this up-close version of me, then I feel like we're giving each other gifts: They give me their attention, and I put myself on the line—both metaphorically and literally—for them."

—**Sarah Rosenthal**, poet and author

Lights, Camera, Action!
Filling Seats at Your Slam

Unfortunately, when a lot of people think of poetry readings, they imagine a smoke-filled room with über-cool hipsters dressed in berets and sweaters nodding appreciatively to a two-hour poem about the beauty of tall weeds. So you may have to do some aggressive advertising at first to get people to attend your slam. If you make really colorful flyers to post at your school that emphasize the fun and competitive nature of the event, it'll help to shake poetry's sometimes stuffy image. Talk to people in person about it, and explain how fun it is. Ask the school paper to write something about poetry slams in general, and your event in particular. Do mini-slams outside during recess to show people how entertaining and lively they are.

Eventually, you won't need to work so hard. Once your friends have attended one slam, they'll want to come again—maybe even participate! That's why it's important to keep the event rowdy, fun, spontaneous, and entertaining. **Remember: This should be a party for words, not a serious classroom lecture.**

"The most important thing I've learned doing poetry slams is that numbers don't mean anything. How I feel is how I feel regardless of what anyone else has to say."

—**Luara Venturi**, 17, Youth Speaks poet

¢ Selling Out Without Selling Out:
How to Raise Funds

An obvious way to raise money would be to charge admission to the slam, but the charge should be minimal, since you want as many people as possible to come. You can also sell drinks and baked goods at the event itself. It helps to put people in a good mood if they've got a plate full of cookies in front of them, and you'll earn spare change to help pay for space rental, prizes, or any other costs associated with putting on the slam.

$1

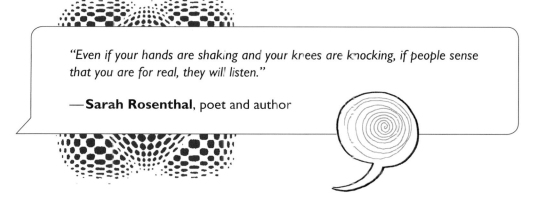

"Even if your hands are shaking and your knees are knocking, if people sense that you are for real, they will listen."

—**Sarah Rosenthal**, poet and author

9 make a PARADE

It's very important to know ahead of time exactly what you want to do for your float, and to plan accordingly. Often, you'll be working with a tight budget—or even no budget at all—and figuring out the effect you want the float to have by using the materials available can be a challenge. But it also can be fun! I find I'm at my most creative when I have to figure out, say, how to make a 10-foot dragon with eight boxes of tissue and a case of toilet plungers.

—**Jill Havagesse**, float designer for Gay Pride and St. Patrick's Day parades in San Francisco

Elbow, Elbow, Fist, Fist

You're standing on a curb with your parents for hours, waiting for the weary marching band to drag itself by, the members wearing weak smiles and scorching hot uniforms. If you're lucky, someone throws a handful of candy at you, but you're too old to fight with the little kids over a Tootsie Roll. An endless line of half-hearted floats rolls by advertising real estate agencies and car insurance companies. Does this scene sound familiar to you? If so, it's no wonder you fear and dread parades.

But parades are not meant to merely be lame events that signal the opening of yet another Bargain Bob's Big Bargain Store. They are about bringing community together to party! You probably know this already if you live in or have visited a city where there are amazing Chinese New Year parades, Thanksgiving Day parades, St. Patty's Day parades, Gay Pride parades, and parades for whatever holiday needs celebrating.

Good parades are not dronelike; they have wild dancing, fantastic costumes, rock bands, amazing floats, and even fireworks. The Saint Stupid's Day Parade on April Fool's Day consists of a lot of people in wacky costumes making noise and acting like morons on purpose. What could be more fun than that?

"But wait," you say, "what about floats? Don't professionals make those things?" Truth is, you and your friends can easily make a float out of basic materials like chicken wire, papier mâché, and tissue paper. Or you can drive a ride-on lawn mower festooned with some flags.

You don't need to wait for a gaggle of homemakers or working stiffs to host the next parade in your town or neighborhood. With a little organization, some good friends, and the right permits, you can be gliding down Main Street in no time.

What You'll Need

✓ a parade route
✓ float construction materials (wood, chicken wire, papier mâché)
✓ costumes
✓ parade permit
✓ tools

CHICKEN WIRE

"One of our major obstacles each year is staying on track and completing our timelines. It is essential that everyone get their job done when they say they will get it done in order for everyone to move on with their respective project ... At times dealing with the paper-work or materials on a deadline can become very stressful. But remember: It's all about the fun!"

—Janetta McDowell, senior coordinator for the Rose Float at California Polytechnic State University

RESOURCES

www.valleydecorating.com
This is a store that sells lots of float-making supplies. More important, it also has a cool tutorial on making your own floats.

www.macysparade.com
Check out this site for one of the most famous parades—the Macy's Thanksgiving Day Parade —to get ideas for your own.

First Things First:
What Kind of Parade?

If you want to have a parade, it helps to have a reason for it. But that's easy—there's always a reason for a parade. Did your local WNBA team just win the championship? Or maybe a new park just opened around the corner. Or the sequel to your favorite movie is arriving. You could also come up with something sillier and more exotic, like The Nacho Cheese Sauce Appreciation Parade. **You can even start with a traditional holiday parade and add your own spin, like a Halloween "Living Dead" Parade or the "Bluegrass" Thanksgiving Day Parade.** Just pick a theme that inspires people to sport some offbeat costumes and construct a cool float.

It's not absolutely essential, but try to make your parade something that will happen annually. The first time around, people may have a hard time believing you can really pull it off and refrain from putting a lot of effort into a float or dance routine. But if you stage a successful parade, even if it's small, other people will want to join in the following year.

Gathering the Troops:
Who Will Walk the Walk

You have your theme and some basic plans. Now you need some paraders. To recruit them, post and hand out flyers in your neighborhood, talk to people you know, and pass out sign-up sheets at local clubs, in classes, and anywhere you go. A surefire way to get people involved is to turn the parade into a contest and offer prizes for things like best float, best costume, and best performance.

Your fellow paraders need not necessarily know what they will do in the parade when they sign up—there are tons of jobs, and there is no such thing as having too many people to work on a parade as you are going to need a lot of (wo)man-power to pull it off. **It would probably be a good idea to form a little committee of your most enthusiastic supporters to help delegate important tasks.**

In the parade itself, people can participate simply by walking along dressed as a duck and playing a tuba, or they can do something as complicated as gliding through the crowd in a palatial float that they built out of papier mâché, a lawn mower, and a bunch of old shoes. People may decide to decorate their family car and wave out the window as they cruise by—this works especially well in a convertible or vintage car. Some people like to unicycle, others form roller-skating troupes. Think about involving the local **skateboard army**, **dance troupe**, **rock band**, or **choir**.

Make sure to rally some adult support because you'll need their help to organize the parade and build floats. If someone's mom or dad is a construction worker or stagehand at the local theater, get them to help with the building. Try local woodshops and the carpenter's union to see if they will donate time to help. People always like pitching in for a parade!

You should plan on being especially nice and helpful around the house for at least a month before the parade so that your family will let you use their cars for your floats, loan out their lawn mowers, and give you a hand in general. Of all the projects in this book, the parade is the most in need of parental involvement. Everyone should nail down some sort of commitment from their parents.

INSIDER TIPS
Eyes on the Prize

If you don't have enough money to get traditional trophies or plaques for the contest award winners, come up with some more creative ways to dole out prizes.

- Ask local businesses to sponsor the parade by supplying a few free gift certificates or other prizes like trophies or flowers (in exchange, give them a nice spot in your parade).

- Create handmade art pieces to give out.

- Offer a service (like a free car wash or a month of dogwalking).

Who's On Board?

Every parade needs:

organizer
the person who brings together all the elements of the parade

float designers/builders
the people who make the floats

drivers for floats
if you've got a license, you can do it; if not,
ask parents and older siblings and friends

musicians
every parade needs music!

contest judges
the people who choose the winning floats, costumes, and more

party organizer
the person who plans the end-of-parade party

Leader of the Pack:
Build It, and They Will Come

Organizing a parade takes a lot of energy and persistence. You have to get permits, remind people of deadlines, and put the word out. Most people will probably see the parade as a great chance to have fun and be creative, without realizing how much needs to be done. Try to delegate any small tasks and do the essential things like meeting permit deadlines yourself, at least for the first parade. Once people get hooked on the idea of having the parade every year, they'll be more reliable.

You may also run into some static at first from your parents, as they will have a hard time believing that a teenager is capable of organizing such a big event. Also, adults outside of your family in the business and political world may be reluctant to deal with a "kid" when it comes to issuing permits and the like (and some big businessmen may give you even more grief because you are a girl). Just patiently keep working away, and eventually adults will realize that you're for real.

Getting Started:
Selecting Your Route and Securing a Permit

So, you've got all these people eagerly waiting to parade down the street hauling balloons, dancing to reggae, and wearing giant sunflowers in their hair. But what street?

As soon as you have some people and ideas together, talk to city hall about permits and any other permissions you might need to hold a parade, especially if there's going to be music or any other loud noise. If you're having it in the street with vehicles, you'll need permits for closing down the street. If you don't want to bother with permits, you could also have the parade on the sidewalk, but you'd have to modify your floats so they don't operate with cars (and you still might need a permit, especially if you have a lot of people).

Choose a route that is big enough that people will be able to see your parade, but not such a busy street that the local government will hesitate to give you permission. A lot of residential neighborhoods will have a broad avenue that doesn't have a lot of traffic, especially on weekends. Be sure to research ahead of time by staking out a spot on the street and watching how much traffic goes by during your chosen parade time. The less traffic, the more likely it is that you will be given a permit. If you find a nice government official, she may even suggest routes for you.

♠ Tricks of the Trade:
It Doesn't Really Float, Does It?

The crowning jewel of any parade, of course, is the float. This can be as simple or as elaborate as you want it to be. Each person along the route is going to experience your float as it passes, so you need to consider how you want people to feel when they see it. Do you want them to laugh? Do you want to say something about issues that affect the neighborhood or the world? Do you want to commemorate someone or something that is important to you? Your float can be a giant guitar, a colorful soccer ball, or a big papier mâché animal. For your first float, choose something simple. It doesn't have to be a perfect reproduction of downtown New York, complete with animatronic people. It just has to be something you'll enjoy working on for a while and that will make a lasting impression on the crowd. Here are some basic things you'll need for any float.

Locomotion

Your float, of course, has to move. You can fill up your little brother's Radio Flyer with statues of feminist punk rockers and drag it along, get behind the wheel of a golf cart full of balloons, or simply use a ride-on lawn mower as your float's transportation. If you have access to a car, hook up a flat-bed trailer to it and build a great float on the trailer.

Construction Materials

The two main construction materials you need are wood and chicken wire.

Wood. You'll need wood to build the base of the float. You can also build a little stage to stand on with more wood. If the float will be carrying people, and it's either in an open truck or trailer bed, you'll need at least one wood post or another secure spot for them to hold onto. A good idea is to build a solid post into the wood frame or stage. You can also lash a post to the truck, but whatever you do just make sure no one is standing without stability.

CHICKEN WIRE

Chicken Wire. A classic way to build shapes on a float is with chicken wire, which is basically a net made out of wire. You can bend this net into all kinds of shapes. Then, to cover it, you can tie pieces of cloth to it or papier mâché it. You can also pinch together the end of a sheet of tissue

INSIDER TIPS
The Art of Papier Mâché

Papier mâché is basically French for "chewed up paper," and it's the perfect material for a float. It is used to cover a shape made by chicken wire. Here's how to do it.

- Tear a lot of strips of newspaper.

- Add one part white flour to every two parts water in a large bucket.

- Mix the goop until it's nice and smooth.

- Dip strips of newspaper in the paste and apply to the chicken wire. Smooth each strip as you lay it down, and add several layers for strength. Make sure it's completely dry and hard before doing anything else with your creation.

papier mâché

If you want to add more shapes that aren't directly part of the chicken wire frame, you can make them out of cardboard. Then attach them, using string or wire, to an area where chicken wire was left exposed, or glue them to the wood frame or posts.

You can also use balloons to make difficult round shapes. Just cover a balloon in papier mâché and pop it once the papier mâché has dried, and you have your round design!

You can paint papier mâché however you like, just make sure it is fully dry before doing so—24 hours should do the trick.

paper, stuff it into a hole, and branch it out. If you do this for several of the holes, you can cover the whole float with tissue paper.

Decorations. These can be pretty much anything you want. At the Rose Parade in Portland, Oregon, the floats are covered either with real roses or roses made out of tissue paper that are attached to chicken wire frames. Tin foil makes a great metallic covering over papier mâché or chicken wire. Letters cut out of construction paper can form phrases important to you, like "Keep on Dreaming" for a Martin Luther King Day parade. The phrase can then either be tied to chicken wire or glued to the wood frame. Cover the whole float with papier mâché and then paint it. Basically, anything you can dream up belongs on a float.

When it comes to building your float, it's perfectly fine (and recommended even) to get people who know what they're doing to help. But that doesn't mean you should let other people build it for you. If you are super lucky, you have an older relative who taught you how to swing a hammer, even though you are "just a girl." If you are like the majority of girls, those lessons were doled out to your brothers and male cousins and a toolbox is as mysterious to you as the big hunk of metal under the hood of the car. Don't be discouraged!

Girls *can* build stuff, and this is a perfect opportunity to hone your skills. Be part of the process completely. Ask for help when you need it, but do as much of it as you can on your own (with your girlfriends, of course). **There are few things quite as satisfying as building something with your own two hands**, and it's a feeling that a lot of girls never get to experience because those jobs get scooped up by the boys in the room.

Lights, Camera, Action!
Planning for the Big Day

Once you have everything built, it's showtime. Putting together a papier mâché forest on the back of a lawn mower is only half of the fun. Now it's time to set the parade in motion. Because it's such a big performance, there are a few things you'll want to do beforehand.

Rehearse

It's best to think of your float or band or dance troupe as moving artwork or even theater, so you should have your "act" down for the big day. **Give everyone in your group a chance to try out their dance moves, songs, and rock 'n' roll salutes at least once before the actual parade.** Encourage other groups joining the parade to practice, too, including any musical acts. Playing music and walking at the same time is harder than it looks.

Set the Order

You'll need to decide which float comes after which marching band comes after which dancing chicken. Make sure everyone knows their number and help them get to the right spot at the start of the parade.

Party Time

It's not always part of a parade, but a fun thing to do is hold a party at the end for all of the participants. Or a big barbecue for the whole neighborhood. Designate someone to organize this part of the parade separately—you'll have enough to think about!

¢ Selling Out Without Selling Out:
How to Raise Funds

There are several ways you can raise funds for a parade. You obviously can't charge admission for folks who are watching the parade, but you could charge a small fee for those who participate in the parade (very small—you don't want to discourage people from signing up). A more common way that parades raise money is by asking a local business to sponsor it. Allow them to have a float or car advertising their business, or even have their name on your flyers, in exchange for a sum of money that they donate. Try to choose businesses that you like or that you think go along with the theme of your parade.

"I love the teamwork involved in making a float. When I'm working with a client and my assistants, we become very close. Parades are all about community, and when we're working on a float we become a little community of our own."

—**Jill Havagesse**, float designer for Gay Pride and St. Patrick's Day parades in San Francisco

About the Contributors

Arne Johnson has been a film journalist and filmmaker for nearly 10 years. Most recently, he collaborated with Shane King on the feature documentary *Girls Rock!*, which has been screened at several film festivals around the world—including the 2007 Hot Docs Film Festival and the Seattle International Film Festival—and opened in theaters in March 2008. He was also an editor on the documentary *Out of the Poison Tree*, a movie about one woman's journey back to the killing fields of her Cambodia homeland, and is currently producing the feature documentary *Cartoon College*. He is a partner in (your name here) productions and has written for *The Onion*, *San Francisco Bay Guardian*, and the *San Francisco Examiner*.

Karen Macklin is a San Francisco-based writer, editor, and teacher. She has written for more than a dozen publications nationally, including *The New York Times*, *San Francisco Weekly*, and *Yoga Journal* on arts, culture, travel, health, and Eastern spirituality. She holds an MFA in creative writing from San Francisco State University and her creative works, which include plays and poetry, have been produced and published in the United States and Italy. She has traveled and lived all over the world, and spent 2006 teaching journalism in Guatemala City as part of a State Department fellowship. She loves working with teenagers and helping to empower young people.

Michael Wertz has been a commercial artist since 1995. He has created work for *The New Yorker*, the *De Young Museum*, and the San Francisco International Film Festival. He lives in Oakland with husband Andy and dog Olive. You can see more of his work at *www.wertzateria.com*.